Climbing Lightly Through Forests

Climbing Lightly Through Forests

A Poetry Anthology
Honoring Ursula K. Le Guin

Edited by
R.B. Lemberg and Lisa M. Bradley

Aqueduct Press
PO Box 95787
Seattle, Washington 98145-2787
www.aqueductpress.com

Publishing histories provided in Reprint Credits, p. 165

First Edition, First Printing, January 2021

ISBN: 978-1-61976-197-1

Library of Congress Control Number: 2020951642

Book and cover design by Kathryn Wilham
Cover photo courtesy Russ Moore
Printed in the USA by McNaughton & Gunn

Land Acknowledgments

I worked on this book from my home in Iowa, the Land between Two Rivers. Iowa has been the homeland for many independent nations: Ioway, Otoe, Omaha, Ponca, Sioux, Sauk, and Meskwaki (Sac and Fox Tribe of the Mississippi). By force and by colonialist treaties, the US acquired the entirety of land in Iowa. Only the Meskwaki Nation, the Red Earth People, managed to purchase land and still maintain sovereignty in the state. Place names like Wapello, Tama, Sioux City, Black Hawk County, and many others remind me daily that colonialism is a destructive, ongoing process. May telling these truths be a small step toward reconciliation.

—Lisa M. Bradley, Iowa City, IA, March 2020

I did most of my editorial and writing work on this book in Lawrence, Kansas. This town is the ancestral homeland of several nations—the Kaw, Osage, and Shawnee peoples, who were relocated by force in the nineteenth century. Today, Kansas is home to many Indigenous people, including the four federally recognized nations: The Prairie Band Potawatomi, the Kickapoo Tribe of Kansas, the Iowa Tribe of Kansas and Nebraska, and the Sac and Fox Nation of Missouri. Lawrence, Kansas, is the home of Haskell Indian Nations University, a federally operated tribal university that was founded in 1884 as a residential boarding school for Indigenous children, many of them forcibly removed from their homes. This is on my mind as a migrant now living in a place with rich, painful, and vibrant Indigenous presence and history.

—R.B. Lemberg, Lawrence, KS, April 2020

Editorial Acknowledgments

R.B.: I am grateful to Bogi Takács, my spouse, for eir help, encouragement, and good advice at various stages of this project. And I'm grateful to Lisa for sharing this work with me—it's been a sheer delight to edit with you. Thank you to the wonderful LGBTQIA+ writers at the virtual pub. Special thanks to my Patreon supporters, who followed along as the process unfolded. Last but not least, I'm grateful to my child Mati for fuzzy hugs and letting me work from time to time.

Lisa: Yes, big thanks to Bogi for crucial input and to our friends at the pub for inspiration and support. We are immensely grateful to Timmi and Aqueduct Press for championing inclusive, feminist SFF. Special thanks to Eileen Gunn for helping us include JT Stewart's work. R.B., thanks for sharing this journey with me (also, stop making me blush). Most of all, gracias a mi familia: José Jimenez, who counters my neurotic rambling with patient reason, and our child, Ash, who understands me even when I can no longer "word."

Contents

2. REBELLIONS   23

Not An Introduction

Lisa: I'm on record as hating introductions. I'm an impatient reader who wants to dive right into the author's work. As an editor, however, I feel the best anthologies are conversations, and newcomers to a conversation often appreciate having some context before joining in. As a tribute anthology, *Climbing Lightly Through Forests* gathers multiple conversations: the poets are responding to Ursula K. Le Guin, her work, or their own responses to her or her work; and as editors, R.B. and I put the poets in conversation with each other and with the readers. So let's begin as we wish to proceed, not as an introduction but as a conversation. R.B., tell me about Ursula's influence on your life.

R.B.: Her work has meant so much to me over the years. *The Left Hand of Darkness* was a revelation and a lifeline for me as a queer, nonbinary, and then-closeted immigrant teen; I read it first in Russian translation. In 2010, I founded *Stone Telling Magazine*, a speculative poetry venue named after the main character in *Always Coming Home*. I approached Ursula to let her know about the new magazine and asked if I could reprint one of her poems. She wrote back with a new poem, "The Elders at the Falls," which appeared in the inaugural issue of the magazine. I did not know a lot about Ursula's poetry before that, except that I loved the poems in *Always Coming Home*, but I began to seek her poetry out after that. How about you, Lisa?

Lisa: I came to love Le Guin's work in college, when I aspired to write speculative fiction about philosophy. *The Dispossessed* rocked my world—here was a book serious about political philosophy but with a fascinating science fiction plot and characters I cared about! It was a model for everything I wanted to write. I must've been aware of Le Guin's poetry, but I don't remember seeking it out.

Eventually, my interest in Spanish poetry brought me back to Le Guin. I can read Spanish, but I rely on English translations as back-up. Imagine my delight when I found a translation by Le Guin! Her work gave me the confidence to write about the speculative poetry of an amazing Chilean poet, which you bought for *Stone Telling Magazine*. That was our first collaboration related to Le Guin.

What did you learn from your deep dive into Le Guin's poetry?

R.B.: Much of her poetry felt very personal to me and not nearly as speculative as her fiction; and there was much less engagement with it, from both readers and critics, so I was interested in why that might be. Le Guin herself said her poetry was dismissed because it was written by a novelist; but I am not sure if that is quite true. It's just that her poetry was so much less speculative, and her readers expected speculative works from her—grand feats of imagination, of *naming* what has been silent for long. The magic of her poetry is quieter. It is in the wind and water, the landscape and the trees, whole forests of them. Ursula called herself an arboreal writer, and the title of this book, a line from one of her poems, reflects that.

Lisa: Arboreal! Certainly, Le Guin looms as large as a sequoia for readers of her speculative fiction. But perhaps we should imagine her as a whole forest, because she wrote astutely and passionately about many things in many genres. I agree, spec readers seem nonplussed by Ursula as Poet, probably because her poetry lacks the comforting protocols of much spec fic. Many spec readers shy from contemporary literary poetry, which is how I'd classify Le Guin's work, and so those readers are even less likely to know that Ursula *translated* poetry. Yet it was Le Guin's translation that crystallized my love for her, specifically *Selected Poems of Gabriela Mistral* (University of New Mexico Press, 2003). Mistral was a Chilean educator, diplomat, and poet who won the Nobel Prize for Literature in 1945, and that essay I mentioned from *Stone Telling* was about Mistral. As a Latina, I'm deeply grateful that Le Guin spotlighted Mistral's work. Western literature, and speculative literature in particular, can feel oppressively white. Le Guin's tribute to this amazing woman is a powerful act of inclusion. This anthology continues in that inclusive vein.

R.B.:   Yes, it was wonderful for me to discover the poetic conversations she had with Mistral and other Latinx poets, and her abiding interest in translation. Inclusion has been very important to us as anthologists, and we have been blessed to receive submissions from poets from all ways of life—poets who were readers and who were friends, poets of many ages and genders, poets from different corners of the world. The poems in this book engage with Ursula's legacy from a multitude of perspectives—from the landscape of the Pacific Northwest to family to feminist issues. I am especially proud of how many queer, trans, and nonbinary voices appear in this anthology. So many of us have felt seen and empowered—and some of us also hurt—by her works, which reached beyond cisnormativity towards a more inclusive world.

Lisa: Indeed, this anthology is enriched by the work of poets from all over the world: Greece, Spain, Trinidad and Tobago, Chile, the UK, Australia, Uruguay, and Canada, in addition to the United States, where R.B. and I are located. (We speak more about that in our land acknowledgments above.) As a fan of Le Guin's translation, I'm so pleased to share Lawrence Schimel's translation of a poem by Spanish poet Ana Tapia, here titled "Song of the Guardians of the Rainbow." Several of our poets wrote in English, although it is not their primary language. We are grateful for their generosity and virtuosity.

We've also included work from over a dozen poets of color, many of whom, like me, felt *seen* by Ursula. She may not have always seen us correctly or fully grasped our contexts, but she recognized non-white, non-Western lives and artists. From that recognition, Sofia Samatar, Shweta Narayan, Brandon O'Brien, and others have spun fascinating, sometimes critical discourse.

R.B.:   I love how the poetry in this volume has such a range of tone. Taken as a whole, the resulting book is deeply Ursuline—in its contemplativeness, in its rebelliousness and resistance, in its thoughtfulness, in its sadness and its hope. When I pitched *Climbing Lightly Through Forests* to Timmi Duchamp at Aqueduct, shortly after Ursula passed away, I did not expect how emotionally difficult it would be for me to choose between so many wonderful, heartfelt poems. I am immensely grateful to Lisa, who came on board a bit later. We worked together previously, but not as co-editors; I loved her editorial approach when she worked on poetry for *Uncanny Magazine*'s special issue "Disabled People Destroy Fantasy." Co-editing this book with Lisa has brought tremendous joy to the process and made the book richer and so much more satisfying.

Lisa: I'm so grateful that R.B. invited me to this project. I've learned magnitudes from R.B.'s keen yet sensitive reading, their loving but clear-eyed critique of Le Guin's work. I learned from our poets, as well. We received enough poetry that we could've curated an entire book of sad poems, or nature poems, or poems celebrating Le Guin's fiction or critiquing it, but as "Journey" by Lyta Gold reminds us, "Grief keeps its own timetable." We chose to reflect the poets' kaleidoscopic range, because, although we all grieve for Le Guin, we may be at different stages of grief. Hopefully, no matter where the reader is in their process, they'll be able to find solace and support in these pages. They can join in the conversations.

R.B.: Working on the retrospective essay and rereading Ursula's poems about grief and age and the long, long process of writing, I felt seen and held in this one idea: it's OK to take a long time to create something that is true. Poetry—all creativity—is often a circuitous journey.

When Ursula passed on January 22, 2018, many of us felt that she left us too soon, that she left us when we still so desperately needed her. She was 88. Yet, many of us wanted her to continue. Her work was so vital, so life-changing. We still need her voice. We will keep reading and thinking, talking to her, talking about her, talking about her stories, telling our own stories. After reading and rereading through the body of her poetry for the retrospective essay, I came to feel that she said what she wanted to say—she said all she *could* say. The rest is up to us.

1. Wind and Water

Dear Ursula,

Edmond Y. Chang

—ent
leant
sent

You rode quietly in the back seat of the car.
Your friend Suzy beside you, laughing.
Margaret was driving; you said you liked my mohawk.
We joked about the run-in with the police
On the way to pick you up from the lecture hall
Where you read letters to the ghost of Tiptree.
I, too, got lost in your time travels, starstruck,
Now by your tottered shape and searching mind
As you peered out the passenger-side window,
Starboard, spying a fragment of a store sign.
You chirp, trying on rhymes like hats, a meditation.

—ast
vast
past

A book of yours told me mountains when I was ten.
Decades later it reminds me of promises made,
Then and today, that words are more than their sums,
That the map of the earth is sea and sky and change.
You taught me words are magic, true names,
Old names, strange spellings—wizard, *ansible*,
Forest, lathe, *kemmer*, sparrowhawk, home,
Journey, anarchy, foxtail, mother, Ursula—
The bear, the octopus, the teacher, the guide.
You taught me not to be afraid of dragons,
To play among islands, to never be frugal with hope.

—eth
breath
death

At the hotel, caught open in the lobby, I asked
For a picture with you, and you nodded gently, tired.
At your ear, I bowed, eschewing my heavy hands,
Caught in your gravity as the day wore you down.
Your smile bore the maps and marks of every story,
Hour, and place your imagination ever visited.
My first contact with ancient generosity and keen grace.
A year later, you came again and remembered my hair.
We would never get the chance to break bread
Or take another ride or talk about how the world hurt
Before the vacuum of loss widened the orbit of your star.

Where Are You?

Jo Walton

You are in a house that creaks with the memory of footfalls.
You are in a boat, far out in the Reaches, changing the rules.
You are contemplating a wall, a threshold, a border.
You are crossing a glacier.
You are singing in the darkness the rhythms that rock a child to sleep.
You are naming and claiming and walking and talking
Challenging, balancing, changing and raging.
You are bemusedly watching a cat.
The moon is rising and you are listening to water in the mountains.
You are extending a hand to somebody.
You are accepting praise, awkwardly.
You are pointing out a heron.
You are reading with delight, greedily, like a child under the covers.
You are watching the dragons rising, spiraling, with furrowed brow,
    reconsidering.
You are eating little fried cakes. You are taking pickles to the
    communal barrel.
You are making and shaping and blinking and thinking.
You are finding your way back through a story,
Like banging rocks in a circle,
Like light (no, faster than that), like the necessity of narrative,
Uphill, over broken ice, near a young volcano.
You are at home, or at least, you always know where home is.
That you are dead is grave. That you are gone seems impossible.

Wind Writes the Water

Roger Dutcher

Wind writes the water
Trees glyph the sky
Still we don't understand

Distance, Interval

M.J. Cunniff

When it rains here the ocean spits wood onto the coastline
as if it means to seed the sand.

Orderly blocks of lumber slipped from a logging boom upriver
beach themselves sullenly on the cold sand; and branches
torn from birch and pine by the wind, drowned and bark-scarred;
and, sometimes, the memories of human hands,
fragments of a crashed boat-hull or a painted door.

It takes night and storms to surface them again, but you can tell,
looking at the water, its eagerness, its quickness to refuse.

How terrible to be the ocean and forget the course of rivers
curved by downed trees, back-eddies flowing with
salmon and vegetation, the obscure webs of life
on the seafloor, which feed on wood instead of light—

How terrible to be the driftwood and forget the water
surging through its columns, xylems veining
furiously up into the air, becoming buds and leaves,

becoming necessary interrelation—

And standing on the coastal rocks looking out
at the shadows of motion, it is impossible
for a long moment to conceive of forgetting it

and the world will pulp the paper
and you will wet the ink to write
an explanation for all this, turn the surface
into a type of understanding.

In Latin, *foris*

Christopher Phelps

Foris meant outside.
So the forest was remote;
Was not a scripted park.

Unsorted, the forest
was scattered and riddled.

Musical and peopled
with unknowns.
Restless and unmannered,

the forest was not for reign.
As it happened,

it was *foreign*, fruited
in that same word again:
foris, the ripening dark.

The package mystery
beyond our ken; our kin.

The Forester's Stratagem

Neile Graham

The trees, gone for centuries, ghost
their roots like rivulets into this land,
down and gone, then reappear, masked

as stone. You never know how they dance
and dance, till you circle, pass then pass
to see them bow, touch, secede, their

shoulders blending, their hidden hands
passing codes. Invisible branches flagging
the sky's take-offs and landings: the clouds

dispersed to collect again. It's that sky
you bring home to your own coast
like damp laundry, let it shake, storm, becalm.

While it settles on the high hemlocks,
the land's raw bones subside under the forest's
flesh, where alders start their own in this new rain.

Spiking spires flag the stumps, the deadfalls.
Dragging up with them the old magics
of the prolific land. It's about the wind

scraping the ocean's salt spice up from the waves
to break on the cedars, on your clothes, on your
hair, through your skin—the taste of green,

green, always green underfoot, on every breeze,
the center of every squall and storm.
The forest's mud scent of mud. The rough

cut of evergreen/everstone. So walk around.
Circle them. The dance of rain tapping
its secret formulae into wood rain stone,

stone rain wood; rain wood; rain stone, old
and new tracing veiny spells down your wrists,
down your hands, down your fingerbones.

Redwood Houses

Amelia Gorman

My house creaks again in the night
and I'm comforted by your architecture essays
that explain redwood houses usually do this.

I brought enough haunts with me across the country
that I'm not sure if my life has room for more.

But if the ghost of the *sempervirens* is here,
let it be here. And if it wheezes through the dark
let me remember where I am and what it cost.

My house creaks me to sleep again and again in the night.

Galloping Hooves

Tricia Knoll

> "The grain of a wood is the language of a tree."
> —Ursula K. Le Guin

I have an oak desk
and a zelkova sewing box.
They hold their tongues today.

So too the oak fireplace mantle.
Fir picture frames and pastry boards.
That cherry spoon a cousin carved.
A ruler from grade school.

Their quiet script shows
as growth rings that sucked water,
how the carpenter lined up joins
so that end grains trace
flecks of music notes.

Then, those time signatures
in the nicks from hooves
of black metal stallions I galloped
on the dark mahogany
dining room table burnt
umber from a prairie sun.

For what we never said
at that table fifty years ago—
I pick up a soft rag
and beeswax paste,
rub the tight grain
to lay to rest
what I might have said.

Kudzu

Stephanie Burt

Inglorious, militant,
it overtook our bright
new porch. My father said its stalks

rose "faster than the eye":
like the body I hated then, and hate.
We had to yank
the screen door off its frame and throw it away.

That year, in my favorite novel,
the astronauts had trouble
with a single-minded planet whose nerves were great trees;

it had watched Earth
grow up, and had stored up thoughts
the length of continents,
which, naturally, it took forever to say.

Pacifica/Evergreen

Hal Y. Zhang

California makes me sick now. It's the ocean
spray, smoky blacktop, disapproving aspen—
T cells raging against the prodigal
daughter who is not forgiven, an
autoimmune flare until I scamper
away, inflamed tail between my legs.

I did not desert you for want of a better life.
There is nothing better, nowhere
more temperate and patient,
and maybe that is why I left
for storm-tossed sunless
seasons, masochist that I am.

When/if I come crawling back for good,
will you take me in your gentle
maw by buttery rolls of my
neck, dip me in the sweet
immortal Tahoe waters until I
am scabbed and scrubbed anew?

I will take it as a blessing, rain upon the Sonoran,
pine needle bare soles, heart buried
in La Brea for all my days until
the time comes to walk into the
sea, unsaid words embalming
me within rising salt tides.

The Other Lives

Sonya Taaffe

for R.B. Lemberg

When you held me on the ice
we were living
and when we came together down the snow
we were not dead
and even at stars' distance from one another's minds
we are not ghosts
resting within one shared shadow
like a hand within a hand
holding light.

Of Winter and Other Seasons

Kiya Nicoll

Somewhere in the ice is a man with a woman's face,
Or something both and neither, in the in-between,
Who knows the children of the body and those not,
The silence and the word that breaks it.

Somewhere in the ice is a memory of a world
With pickle barrels on every corner, abundant,
Paradoxes of barren wealth and freedom,
Walls, and reverence for life.

Somewhere in the ice is a voice half-garbled
Pining for mindspeech which cannot lie
In the hope of being understood at last,
Or riding the wind on feline steeds.

Somewhere in the ice is the path that remembers home,
A way which is mother of ten thousand steps,
A place with blankets dyed dirty green,
An imagined recollection of belonging.

Somewhere in the ice is a broken child imprisoned,
Is a woman lost in time with a necklace in her hand,
Is a man wandering the haunted passages of nameless gods,
Is the scope to dream of making another world.

Somewhere in the ice is a mirrored reflection
A hidden hollow pooled between worlds and under trees
A shadow named for itself, and without that glass
How would I have ever become?

"Might as well say I'm the words she read"

Betsy Aoki

Snow glint. Crack of ice under hoof.
Stampede of deer, spooked, down from a trail
to where they become her words for fear,
feed, green and slave. The mind inside the hand
hits. The finger bones of thought glitter.
Capable seamstress, stitching wings and winds to beat
together in this melody, signing a brief name
on the earth to be filled in with rain, oh Ursula
how the words are ever not enough to have met you,
silence from the galactic ansible,
ashes float under a weeping tree.

[The title is a line from Ursula K. Le Guin's poem "Leaves."]

Poet Stumbles upon the Ten Thousand Things

Brandon O'Brien

I open the book for
the door to the hidden
and hope to be eaten by something.
I hear the thing is deep and
I'm just looking for a cavern to
hate myself in unnoticed, to mask
fear under faith until I make it
back out. I find rivers instead,
and they won't let me take my rage with me.
They ask me to put everything down,
they hover their hands around each
fear and kindle them to elements.
They are anechoic when I want to scream.
They make cool mist when I set myself aflame.
They just won't let me want, or boil, or burst at all.
I ask the matron at the foot of them,
who just says, "things flourish, then perish."
She asks if I could be doing
anything but screaming.
I ask if she'd let me dare if
I had an answer, if I could be allowed,
just this once, if this was the book that
I could find fire in. But the whole thing
spoke down to fire. And the more it tests me tempest-livid,
the more it made me milding-mist, and then,
I was something else anyway, just a stone
made smooth by it all, slowly rounding,
one state, then another, like revenge is on one
end of the line, and on the other is cool,
and here I was, slowly, ignorantly,
walking the line.

2. Rebellions

Speculative Fiction

Linden K. McMahon

I want there to be a space commune
named Le Guin. It will be on Earth.
We will tell each other stories at night.
We will believe what we say.

The white rhinos will come back
and rampage through London
putting their horns through car windows
and bellowing songs of triumph.
We will call them dragons, get out of their way,
and leave offerings to them at traffic lights.

I want to walk away
and have something to walk towards:
to make the stony spaces ours,
to learn to grow food
in the most unlikely places.
I want the soil back.

Words will be light and springy.
They will be like reeds
and we will blow through them.
Everything will be a library.

I want the bleached coral to evolve
into something new, to rise
from the sea and tell us:
we must imagine better.

sound science

Hal Y. Zhang

say the perseids. say the greek fire hailing down, the name of ones past our shoulders standing, teeth tinkling distilled ice crystals blooming skin flimsy-thin on water's edge quietly inward into slippery spikes. turn on the safelight and look into the dark, every
single
photon. wait three beats to roll thick wooly thunder underfoot, ever true, through air and ozone and the luminiferous æther of our imaginings. the golden petrichor of bereaved electrons whispers here we are not caretaker
mother
lover
friend. here the taut undrawn trees rise from the static storm of our webbed thoughts and susurrations, and to expire is to lose all limits, implode into shards of starbright for curious children to collect, talismans against the night.

Upwards Toward the Light (a found poem)

Rachel Swirsky

We have nothing but freedom:
not a gift given, but a heavy load
of permanent, intolerable uncertainty
that binds us beyond choice.

To be whole is to be part.
We all have forests in our minds,
unexplored, unending
stories in the middle of living.

When we are finally naked in the cold,
we who are so rich, so full of strength,

we breathe back the breath that made us live,
we give back to the world all we did not do,
we are left only with kindness.

To see how beautiful the Earth is,
accept the responsibility of change,
see it from the vantage point of death.

Physics 6

Ursula Whitcher

Why are we still talking about uncertainty?
We can bend light!

In the basement in the dark we turn our mirrors.
Without a cloud of chalk dust the red beam's
imagined only, but four circles where it strikes.
    We cannot look along it: human eyes
    can focus too much light.
(You spread your hair above me in the sun.)

A pearly length of cable, angles matched
to zigzag miles within the tighter coil.
The yellow atoms burn in place. Believe

we slow light down.

Dream Logic

Ada Hoffmann

1. Mountain: *Obstacle, challenge. Achievement. Determination. Higher consciousness and spiritual truth. A rush for success. To dream of a painting of a mountain signifies struggle ahead.*

I am afraid. I have not slept:
behind my eyes there is a thunder
of waves, slick with undertow.
When I dream, this thing behind me
reaches out into the world,
uproots the state of things,
and I wake in the wreckage.

You will not believe me
when I tell you what I fear.

You may argue, Haber:
debate the semantics of *gift* and *curse*.
Tell me this power should please me.
But the *gift*, if you must name it that,
was given to me.
It is not yours.

*2. **Bear:** Independence, strength, endings/beginnings, life/death/rebirth. Introspection, awakening. Dominant and possessive figures. To dream of a bear emerging from a still pool of water signifies emotional force.*

You reached into me. Took hold of the current
that flows behind my dreaming eyes.
Pushed, with all your will and strength,
in the direction you chose.

No, I said. That is not what I wanted.
Ah, you said. Ah, but this
is better than what you asked.
As walls erupted from the ground
and nameless multitudes choked
on dream-pestilence.

I dream I can say no to you.
I scream in your face. I refuse.
I refuse. I wake, and there you are,
smiling down.

As your edifice rises in iron and glass
and the lights of war yellow the sky.

3. Volcano: *Loss of control. Rage. A damaging outcome. Past issues put to rest. To dream that an eruption destroys a city signifies an argument.*

Pain is not energy. It is not conserved.
You cannot hold it still
as you weigh it on the cosmic scales.
Calculate precisely this currency,
the amount of despair
that is exchangeable for terror,
for agony, squalor, grief.

You cannot wipe all pain from the world.
Though you try, sweeping with your bear-heavy hands.
The soil creeps back in, claiming what is life's,
what is stained and cracked and endures
through change. No matter how
you strain and push, pain survives.

But you will strain—you are that type—
again and again, enraged with effort,
until you rip yourself apart,
and half the world with you.
Good luck digging out
from that avalanche, Haber.
You never understood the dirt.

4. Turtle: *Truth, patience, steady progress. Loyalty. Long life. A shelter from danger. Standoffishness and a facade. To dream of turtles swimming in the sea represents unconscious wisdom.*

It may well be
that my greatness and your victory
both were lies.
See: a current flowed through me,
as the waterfall cleaving
the boulder's imperfection,
pooling down into wide kettle-lakes
and new streams.

It is gone now. The river diverted.
Look at me, Haber:
the rock of me worn and ragged
among the grass and pebbles
of the overgrown bed.

If you had been content with this:
gray-brown roots growing softly down
in the soil you tried to wash away.
Green faces turning,
hesitant, to the sun.

The Trees Are Waiting

Gita Ralleigh

If all along the trees
are waiting, unfurling milk
root to tender earth,
pulsing bright skin come
green summer, letting red
capes fall, lifting bare limb
to sky in gentle
supplication.
All along as
gods laugh, cities fall,
people take arms
against their own—
if all along the trees
are waiting to right things:
wild radicals whispering
soft winds
to storm flung
chorus. If all along
the trees are the
join of sundered
sky and earth.
If all along we'd known,
the trees are waiting.

We Dream the Future in Our Songs

Eva Papasoulioti

You treed your dreams in your lungs, grabbed their roots and weaved them around your throat and legs.

You're too unripe to have seen everything.

Now, walk the path the earth sends you, dream asleep and dream awake, dream your truth and dream your bloom, and when your dreams exhale at last, break into the bark of your ancestors and count the rings of this world in your rhythm.

> If you have to uproot in blood, so that you plant in peace,
> harvester,
> use your nails and teeth and hope
> and pull from dream to world
> with a lullaby.

Your green, growing dreams forested this land, your new songs will turn the leaves towards the sun again.

Atmospheric Inversion

Kim Goldberg

The best thoughts, the ones that could save us, that could mend all
clouds and reformulate blood-dipped bayonets as blades of
grass, these are the ones that are smuggled out as
contraband flints strapped to the underside of houseflies hell-bent for
liberty... Give me wingtime with no flight plan or give me
carrion luggage... Yet even in their absence, I see stabs of
hope, backlit motes of dreamy possibility paddling upstream on
a wishbone raft, small tufts of unslung idea that somehow ducked false
contentment on the rockpile of the herd mind. The butterflies have
disappeared as sacrificial offerings in the crusade against
gypsy moths. Gone are swallowtails, mourning cloaks, apollos,
from scrubbing the landscape raw with gut-blind ethnic
cleansing. My mind is a white room where a washerwoman stoops
from scrubbing the landscape raw with gut-blind ethnic
gypsy moths. Gone are swallowtails, mourning cloaks, apollos,
disappeared as sacrificial offerings in the crusade against
contentment on the rockpile of the herd mind. The butterflies have
a wishbone raft, small tufts of unslung idea that somehow ducked false
hope, backlit motes of dreamy possibility paddling upstream on
carrion luggage... Yet even in their absence, I see stabs of
liberty... Give me wingtime with no flight plan or give me
contraband flints strapped to the underside of houseflies hell-bent for
grass, these are the ones that are smuggled out as
clouds and reformulate blood-dipped bayonets as blades of
the best thoughts, the ones that could save us, that could mend all.

The Keystone Out of Your Arch

Sonya Taaffe

I waited so long for a letter from Sfaroy Kampe
I had to write it myself,
I knew no one
anymore on those limitless roads of stone.
That dry-voiced boy with his year at the Normal School,
unsatisfied as autumn, I recognized him
six years before my own rocks fell,
before I was the one losing fights,
running away.
We traveled the same class then, his imaginary mountains
sliding to salt marsh beyond my northbound train.
Karst underfoot
means a land at the mercy of water,
its silence dissolving, darkness
eating earth's work like time.
I learned to walk on a hard ground of echoes,
listening for the still running rivers,
the unquiet, vulnerable wind.

Tolk

So Mayer

came back & hard. That small
rock denser than, pitted inner
workings of the earth, from that
that beach that tried to end me.
High wind and the sheer shear
of metal too near skin. You read the
book of stone, of waves, and say
these their names. Such tongue
of man is none of mine, Latinate
or dialect. What sea calls stone
is lover. How they shape each other
yes even this shadow green &
cold that thought to drown in. Proud
cliff, invitation, stop off the dance of
breath. Sunset or fire. These islands
seethe with all their heat of making,
still. Swallow seacold water, salt
to burn clean the cuts. Piss hot into
chill; more salt, all salt, this
falling. Stumble up one pebble at a
time. It will take months to write
what reflex knew, to (heart muscle)
release. Release. Call it curse
or cumulation, relative density
metamorphic in this frail geology
(skin thins not in millennia but
years; days; the day when—) That
rock. Its pittings harbour salt, still,

beneath the lick. Some other tongue that
tongues, curled as wave to hold
the name of stone (we think it
permanence, that word, to which
sand, blown in eye replies) & speak—

On the Long Road Back

Aimee Ogden

You will not be expecting us.

When an evening's quiet
reverence invites you to
introspection, you do not
take its hand.

When the night paints
the sky dark blue, you will not
look to the far-off hills and you will not
see us there.

Our feet and backs weary but
our chests churning with questions
whose answer we may yet build
and our minds afire with the memory of
a child
(our child).

When the mountain passes
thaw so too will our aching
home-starved hearts.

You would see us if
you look hard enough into
the darkness. You would
hear—if you strained—the
rhythm of our labored
breathing, our heavy footfalls.

Hurrying homeward in search
of something better that we but
dimly understand and that
you dare not examine.

You will not be expecting us, but
we are
walking back.

The Day before the Revolution

Izzy Wasserstein

We've survived worse, they say.
I wonder who they mean by we.
Everywhere I look, stars
& stripes snap in the summer wind.
Police patrol streets. ICE trucks
roll with escorts. Each day I choose
to rise, to struggle, to write a few words.
Each day it grows harder.

I am no good at belonging.
If *I* must be part of *we*,
Let it be we who believe
we might yet grow a better future,
that Anarres or something better,
something queerer, awaits.

I worked my whole life for a revolution
that never came, the elderly man
told me, many years ago. He was not mourning,
but grim-faced, unflinching.

Belong, v.: to be property of.
I belong to no one, or
I belong to those who may come after me,
who will keep my story alive
or let it die according to whim or chance.

There are so many who did not survive,
who ended in AIDS wards, in camps,
broken upon shores, abandoned in prisons,
frozen on streets, bombed, starved,
shattered in alleyways, killed for lack of insulin,

murdered by cops, dead by their own hands.
I believe in Anarres, but I won't live
to see it. There may be a revolution,
but many may not survive,
will not survive. We are those obliged
to tend the garden they planted,
to cultivate what others may yet harvest.

3. Bodies and Boundaries

Icarus

Thoraiya Dyer

That helicopter, sound-mouth
with bullet eyes
flies,
the ordinary world
rushing up behind.

A single feather slips between
its teeth, uncut,
but all of me would crack,
axe-felled,
to bone-splinter red rain,
if I could not grow Ursula's wings again.

Catch the wind, throw it behind.
Snowballs of white cloud, flung
to stay ahead
of roar, and strafing lead.

In and out
of pink lungs, my air
is left behind to be spun, funneled.

But I am not there.

From the Ansible, a Voice

Charles Payseur

Hello?
We are so very far and yet
there too I hear the seasons changing
and perhaps the squirrels are out, gray black white red
(like here)
or purple green sky blue
busy paws dig-jump dig-jumping
to the music of jay and oriole and redwing blackbird.

where the rivers cut cliffs into hillsides
and lazy trails are interrupted
by storm drain waterfalls
there waits a place for illegal dumping
mattress graveyard haunted by broken televisions
with a single perfect doorframe
half buried in trash.

I swear I heard a voice defiant as the sun in winter
just a moment ago, now gone
and I want to say
something
thankful perhaps
(or in any event profound)
but look, all I have are the flickers of diving loons
beneath the crystal shadow of the water
and the strange call of cranes
like alien landscapes
in sound,
all disrupted by a distant shotgun's retort.

Please, are you there?
If we both reveal the worlds around us
then maybe we will find
where we are
in relation to each other.

If I could give lie to all the hurt around me I would say
there is a monarch aflutter against the screen,
something beautiful and fragile
(and fitting)
    But here, the translator, try this instead,
    that for every quaver in my voice
another forest is burning
another world
and word.

Something is breaking
through the fog of intent
across the distance between stars
and you
    and me.

    good bye, good bye,
the seasons are changing
but at least we have these voices
cast out past where arms can embrace
and even if they come back static
(tomorrow)
even if
a line
goes

we will hold a memory
like a seed, and new voices
spread across the inky galaxy
will still fill the space between worlds
with something more than darkness.

The Topography of Ambition

Wendy Howe

"All we have is means."
—Ursula K. Le Guin

It's the road that cuts through everything
sparing what little it can
of grassland and woods, the personal property
of farm and heart.

Yet, somewhere en route, the regrets
keep drifting in. Their exhalations spent
like milkweed over stalk or bush. But in one tree
the conscience sings. A vocalist with an old guitar
strumming an old ballad

about love and sacrifice, the moan of sea gulls
(after a storm) and a fisher girl stooping in the tide
to scavenge what's ever left.

Frost Ascending

Kendra Preston Leonard

When I am old, I shall become Frost,
and cover the trees and grass;
and red berries I will bring forth,
to sate my appetites.

I shall wear thorns of ice
and pearls of the wild sleeping waters;
I will be girded with flowers of steel;
I will stride across worlds.

Ossify

Jennifer Mace

when ice settles deep
into the crackling bones
of the earth, will you
come to me? with your hands
like lightning, will you
lift me up from slumber,
coax my sinews into song,
will you split open my ribcage
like a geode?

I am waiting. lichen creeps
across my cheekbones, down
the knobbled ridge of my spine. it
lives bitterly, stubbornly, imposing
a spiteful beauty on neglect.

like tumbled stone, I allow myself
to be reclaimed. the thatch has fallen.
birch saplings sprung of puddled sun
tear open the hearth of me. ivy,
brown with patience, presses tendrils
through the pores of my skin, infiltrates
the red sluggish rivers of my veins,
insinuates a sort of longing
for the sky.

and have you won? is this
a waking, this geological shift,
as mountains, born by glaciers,
reach the sea? I am igneous

with grief, calcified and fossilized
and knit of things colder
than stone. you will not find me
here.

Keepsake

A.J. Odasso

Writing on the body, always writing on the body, always stories on bodies I am fighting to keep alive, fictional bodies, real bodies, *my body*; bodies betrayed by their stories, *always*, bodies in broken fictions and in realities where they don't belong, words and pictures needled ink-scrawled blood-blurred *scarred*; if only I could keep them safe, if only I could keep them from ruin, if only I could keep you, *if only*.

Gebbeth

A.Z. Louise

I wax and wane with the fullness of
dark gorge black until I purge and am
little more than a vessel for pure
hunger

What do you wait for,
Shadow?

The sweet-soft ooze of molasses
despair slaking the thirst of centuries

What do you wait for,
Shadow?

I crave what slows under the weight of
time the light that burns to nothing eating
itself alive at my touch

What do you wait for,
Shadow?

The last spark yawns me open to mother
void her ocean strength soaking soul-deep

A Headful of Hair

Leah Bobet

Eventually you learn people were always rivers; to hold
them with fingers spread wide. After timewith slow things—
tree branches interlacing, a hospital day sifted to heartbeats,
small hands learning loaf-shapes as the dough firms—you learn
love like a dandelion seed, balanced, balancing on your palm.

Push out the boats, test the tides, greet the dawn: there is
always good fishing on the weir. You can draw up your dead
drifting seaward if the winds are right. Cast it forth: a net woven
of your own living hair, and their voices will flow where plait and
tangle part—just a touch, dandelion seed, seaweed against your palm.

We all live on the water: seep through lovers' turns of phrase uncontained,
in how she salts stock before the meat goes in; woven into our hair,
light and living, dead ends reaching, still slowly growing, and balanced
like fingers spread wide.

When I go, I want a headful of hair streaming behind me forest-thick,
a delta wild and full as the day I was born—unschooled in separation,
loud, unshy, languageless, grasping too hard—and was delivered,
overflowing, into unmapped arms.

Evening (terza rima)

Susannah Mandel

I don't know anything about this rain.
How could I tell you when to take the washing
in? Nor you nor I can read the stain

of color that spreads on these strange, high, thin
cloud forms at suns' set, nor the drift behind
the smells in this thick air. We must again

learn to read, as do children, this new wind
and sky.
            But you have me, as I have you,
for language model: learning how to find

the sense in the almost-familiar, halfway changing, ever new.

And So if You Go Down, You Go Down Whole

Jeannelle D'Isa

After "The Fliers of Gy," *Changing Planes*

We have no
gods with wings. No word
like *angel.*
What we know
is the fever of bodies,
bones, made new for flight.

No one asks.
We don't write this down.
Alar bones,
all our bones,
lie like strangers', and our skin
seeks not touch, but the whole air.

If we fly—
one in a thousand—
our wings fail.
Out at sea
who will know we dreamed of flight?
"Doesn't everyone?"

ode to illness

Gwynne Garfinkle

> "You will find yourself—as I know you already have—in dark
> places, alone, and afraid."
>
> —Ursula K. Le Guin,
> "A Left-Handed Commencement Address"

I long to leave myself behind
to rollick impervious

in my own summer festival
all sunlight and blithe dancing

oh to abandon the tedium
of suffering

the weight of things I never
thought I'd have to endure

not just to heal
but to obliterate

all consciousness of the body
(in)articulate in its pain

instead I must open the door
go inside the darkened room

hold close my fearful
and diminished self

The Place Where We Don't Touch
(To Therem Harth rem ir Estravan, from Theirs to Thine)

Xian Mao

This moment between us, precarious as an icicle in spring
I hold it in my hand and it does not melt
My heat is foreign to it
My heat is foreign to you.

Stranger, you come here proclaiming of "I" and "Thou"
Yet you do not allow us to name ourselves
Not our bodies, in kemmer which you call "heat"
No time given for the other days of our lives
I do not question what you call us in your mind
What linguistic gauntlets you must be running to conceptualize my body
Are you worried of the words your mind may inadvertently speak?
Are you worried I might hear you?

But what words have I called you, Genly
When I still cannot pronounce your name
I have been thinking about your planet, trying to turn your stories into
    feeling
You touch me and help me imagine summer
I never realized your planet was so intemperate
Or how winter was so closely linked with death
Not sleep or quiet, not home
If you can accept your planet's ever-changing climate
Can't you see my body as a body of seasons?

The stalactite is an icicle that doesn't melt
The stalagmite lies beneath it to catch its promise

This divide between us, what are we afraid of?
Perhaps it is time for us to discover spring.

An idea of boundary

Shweta Narayan

What the rains left: light unbalanced,
un-shadowed, a human male among human
beings who were (flinch
from the first slur to fall guard-down on Genly's) neuters, his
landlady (a voluble man), neu- lunar changelings deviant (-ter)
                              —I've
                         reached
wordless from skyshore, tiptoe
pulling her worlds from their high shelf. I've swayed
searching (cold unbalanced) for ways in, walltops
she'd never write. Climb,

slip (breathless in space-cold air), search
both ways for belonging, fall. Climb (scabs torn), slip
to another world, wall, always (-euter) climb. How do we shed
callouses
grown round her sharp edges? Still breaks skin, her neu-(flinch)
slashed in icelight afterimage whose betrayal
was of a friend. All I had: her marginal world,
on the edge. Her lunar alien, my person
sprawled on that border breathless, chest
half shot away, misgendered
even then. My people die.

All I had: two biting edges, weathered
for the unwritten perch. Can I break orbit
from icesight unhumaning to fall (speak)
soft-edged with white-winged crows into dusk, suckle
sky-cow thunder, scatter on warm rain, reach
through (neut-) unbelonging for a landshore
of pandan walls eaten by river-silt? What beloved aliens
would I find? How

did we misplace a city?
What the rains left: unbalance, icebright
neut- (no) slipping through Genly's binary gaze
and hers, learning
to (shed, rewrite) dance on star-grit salt, ungendered,
many-headed, outside words, to leave
scale-prints, edge-blurred launch-prints,
shadowed, tentative, loyal
for your flight.

Concern (a found poem)

Brandon O'Brien

This is a rendition. I do not know any Chinese. I
approach at all because in 1898
each character followed a
transliteration; it is unending.
To have text accessible was not only a stone
itself, but a touchstone for
one another. I focus on word
interpreting, I understand choice,
I compare and see varied
tremendously; sometimes bias
was included; discover several
meanings the same. And finally, for all
my ignorance, I gain intuition,
cadence, conscience.

Without access to text, I would have
been defeated by differences,
following them towards a version. It was
working to lead me into always
knowledge, decisions, light in
darkness.
When you try to follow, even if you wander, good
things you do not deserve work.
I started with few.
I bit, I'd sit and really
get the undeserved good thing, true,
genuine, ancient,
saw some bits scurvily quoted by myself,
asked for more. I do not get into
teaching, I encourage, I can say only
the end:

don't hoard;
do for others,
give richer.

The Brown Thing

Sofia Samatar

Recently, I read that the word *bear* means "the brown thing." Long ago in the forests of my language, people were so afraid of the bear they wouldn't say its name. At last they forgot that name, and so a bear became simply *bear* and I was left with only this word and a feeling of something escaped in the darkness, at large.

You who knew the difference between a name and what something is called: I write you this letter on red paper.

In my dark house I read your imaginary translations. Your "Fragments from the Women's Writing," written after you read about a Chinese linguist's discovery of nüshu, the women's script. In the introduction to the poem, you describe this script, used exclusively by the women of Jiangyong in Hunan, a script that resembles oracle bone carvings of the sixteenth century B.C.E., that might be a relic of writing systems forbidden upon the unification of China, an unofficial, fugitive language, reserved for women's songs, autobiography, and letters between sworn sisters, which you called *the other grammar*, and which you made, in your poem, a revolutionary, prophetic code in which a woman declared the *Empire will fall.*

Something prowls about my house. The evening of the year. On the black window, a few stars, wan as if written in milk.

How to keep the awareness of lost names? This was one of your questions. How can you remember what is hidden? In the introduction to your poem, you mention (gentle caution) that since you wrote it, *genuine translations* of nüshu have been published. What is the relationship of the genuine to the imaginary translation? Does one cancel the other out? I read that the women wrote on fans. They embroidered mottos on belts and scarves. The last writers of nüshu inscribed it on newspaper with a ballpoint pen. Did you transgress in your poem, should you have left the way clear for the genuine translations, was it a mistake to write

63

the imaginary? This poem whose last line seems to me to contain the seed of poetry itself. *Sister: I am lonely. Write.*

In my dark house I read the genuine translations. I read, W*e went to the street, bought red paper.* I read, *I write this letter myself on a paper fan.* Through so many works of writing you tried to hold two options. Option 1: There is an important difference between genuine and imaginary translations. Option 2: All translations are approximations and therefore imaginary. Option 2 is a matter of philosophy, Option 1 a matter of ethics. I read, *The misery of mother and daughter is found on this fan.*

I write you on this handkerchief. It is a humble gift. We two are the same. We are born under bad elements.

In my dark house a spray of starlight. Faint. The Little Bear. Something prowling. I read of the last proficient writer of nüshu, Yang Huanyi, who died twenty years after your poem was published. The headline: *Language dies with woman.* Is there always another grammar?

You must visit me often so we can console each other.

There is the word *bear* and there is the bear's forgotten name and there is the bear. Writing: a brown thing.

I am fortunate in my name, you wrote once, *and would not be named for any creature I did not fear.*

Archive

The phrases "the other grammar," "the Empire will fall," "genuine translations," and "Sister: I am lonely. Write": Ursula K. Le Guin, "Fragments from the Women's Writing," in *Going Out with Peacocks,* HarperCollins, 1994.

"We went to the street…": from a nüshu poem by Tang Baozhen, translated by Cathy Silber, quoted in Lauren Young, "Remembering Nüshu, the 19th-Century Chinese Script Only Women Could Write," *Atlas Obscura,* 16 February 2017.

"I write this letter myself…" and "The misery of mother and daughter…": from a nüshu poem by He Huanshu, transcribed by Zhao

Liming and translated by Julia T. Broussard, quoted by Broussard in "*Nüshu*: A Curriculum of Women's Identity," *Transnational Curriculum Inquiry*, vol. 5, no. 2, 2008.

"I write you on this handkerchief..." and "You must visit me often...": nüshu writing, author unknown, translated by William Wei Chiang, quoted in Lin-Lee Lee, "Pure Persuasion: A Case Study of *Nüshu* or 'Women's Script' Discourses," *Quarterly Journal of Speech*, vol. 9, no. 4, 2004.

"Language dies with woman": *The Observer*, 26 September 2004.

"I am fortunate in my name...": Ursula K. Le Guin, "Bear," *Parabola*, vol. 8, no. 2, 1983.

4. Kin and Kind

Subjunctivitis (or: a Stratagem of Mortality)

Margarita Tenser

If I am to give birth to myself, Auntie, who will raise me? Living, as we do,
in the muddle of the modern world, atomic selves incentivized and
  algorithmically led to market

who will draw me from my nuclear confinement? In my hive
of urban isolation, I eat stories and ventriloquize myself a village

cut and paste community from fertile time and space to bring me up.
I, by virtue of being mostly a fictional character

or a selection thereof, a patchwork quilt of people each collaged, like all art,
either by themselves or through the eyes and hands and bodies

of whoever does the Work, can picture some great-aunt
to ask for wit and wisdom by the fire — or a forest crone whose hut

to creep beside, hoping to overhear forbidden stories. Speak in many
  voices, tell me I exist
inside a pattern that won't cut me down to fit or strangle me with artefacts

of social systems amberized in golden age delusion. Show me I can be a
  chapter
in a narrative that means something to me, instead of choosing

between suffocation and the void. From the saga ursuline
I draw my chirping old Tiresias to row this patched together boat

across the gulf of the absurd. I like it. Now it's mine.

The Scent of Green

Sandra J. Lindow

"It is good to have an end to journey towards;
but it is the journey that matters, in the end."
—Ursula K. Le Guin,
The Left Hand of Darkness

Green leaves smell green—
the profligate kindness of chlorophyll,
but beyond green there's more,
a subtle botanical bouquet,
its idiosyncratic chemical signature
wafting and weaving
olfactory paths:
maple leaf zap of sap,
rhubarb stem whiff of sour,
Tickweed's faint fragrance: baby's bath soap;
briar patch where black cap nubs
change, faint green to tangerine:
subtle differences, scents of becoming;
late season dandelion leaf,
the peppery scent of success:
green grandmother energy,
focused on roots
now that her kids have gone.
Awash in scent songs,
a sun-spun bumble bee, big
as a thumb, flaneur of foliage,
bumbles with purpose.

Dancing at the Edge

Margaret Wack

Mother of mothers, unlike the pictures,
you do not wear red or blue but a brown
the color of dirt, eat rice with your fingers
and lick bowls dry. In the paintings,
you are a nesting doll, you contain multitudes,
you spit them out like a snake with fangs
of gold. Patron of mothers and children, yes,
but also carpenters: those who build something
out of nothing, arching it up to meet
the sky in a display that can be reverent
or else too bold to stand. Also of childless people,
or those who wish to become childless,
or those precariously with child. Also the makers
of lace, something so fine as to be seen through,
also dealers in old clothes, seamstresses,
stablemen, those who keep or move house.
You don't commit, you have a little, enough,
of that immortal fire left in your breast
for paradox, like God, you are the patron saint
of sea and sailors, also storms.
You have a face like something dug up
from the earth, you are always at the edges
of the stories and the holy books, you are the queen
of apocrypha and poverty and wine, your body
is a dark, wet cave smelling of sulfur,
rich with swollen veins of precious metals.
Your attributes are the books you are not in,
the doors you have not walked through,
the horses you rode bare-legged
through the desert without stopping.

Until the Ships Came

Nicole Field

Tucked between Aeaea and the rocks of Scylla,
There was once a home,
An island
Of flowering meadow,
Plentiful game,
Melodious bird life
And us.
We were the hunters
And gatherers
And weapon makers.
Those who cooked,
Or cleaned,
Or told stories around the fires at night.
There were never too many of us in number,
Nor too few for companionship and work.
We didn't tax the bounties of our island too greatly,
And it gave back to us in return.
For each of us, there was a place
And in our time we fit
Without question
Without worry
Without ever wondering why.
For truth,
We did not see it odd
That our forms shaped all the same,
Not until the ship came.

I first spied them at dawn,
Off in the distance.
By midday, I saw the shape of them more clearly:

A hull decorated with a fleshy figure,
Straining forward and backward
All at once.
They dropped anchor in the soft sand,
Strode ashore as though it was their right,
Whilst we peered on in wonder.
For sure,
We had seen their type before
But never so many
And so unaffected
By the sea that bore them to us.
They grew hair where we did not.
Their voices were deeper.
Their shoulders wider.
But still.
They growled and strutted and postured
In ways that some of us did.
Of a surety, we were not so unlike.
Aglaope was the first to step forward.
"Who is in charge among you?"
Her splendid voice reaching across the sand between us.
And, of them, one stepped forward,
Amidst many raised eyebrows
And confused stares of the companions.
"I am Odysseus, and these are my men."
With the sound of confidence in his voice,
Their own normalcy was restored
While ours remained scattered.
For them, confusion faded to smiles,
Already assured of the willingness they'd find.
We did not know
We did not meet them on equal ground.
We did not know
We weren't the same as them.
We did not know
We would learn a new word that day:

Woman.

It wasn't a word to signify
We were from far across the sea,
With a culture vastly different to theirs.
It was a word to group us all together
To say *we* were all the same
But that *they* were different.
It was word to show where we belonged:
Beneath them.
In their eyes
We saw in ourselves
Something we'd never seen:
Uniformity.
They came to our shores,
And offered us homes, and riches,
As if we couldn't source those ourselves.
For some of us, I can only imagine this appeared as good.
But others
Stood tall
Eye to eye
With those
Who lacked the vision
To see them.
We did not want all the same things
Because of some flesh on our chests,
Or clefts between thighs.
For time uncounted,
We'd lived unburdened
By external gaze
Of people who would view these bodies
As synonymous with wants
And needs.
As we tried to explain,
The future we told
Was a past we'd lived:
Where all people went unjudged

On the shapes they saw;
Where gender was not based
On a body
They'd had no choice inhabiting.
And that flesh
Would not become
The center
Of their internal world.
They did not stay long;
We can be glad, at least, of that.

In the stories they told of us,
We wore wings,
And the bodies of birds,
Whilst they stoppered their ears,
Against our dreaded song.
They stole away our rights,
Reduced our number
And our voices,
Relegated us to myth;
A few short lines
In one man's epic.
Just like that,
We were no longer human,
No longer a challenge
For them to overcome.

But, we'll tell you now:
It was never our song that scared them.
It was the sound of the words we said.

Song of the Guardians of the Rainbow

Ana Tapia
Translation by Lawrence Schimel

Listen, my sisters,
how the blood flows through my hands when I try
to break the chains that hold us captive

our souls have made this journey of invisible ships
toward an inherited servitude
and now
no more Orwell, no more whips, no more ashes
of the hate that still hurts us

we must dance a dance older than mankind
from a time no one still remembers

the past is the future: time will be ellipse

my sisters
let the hyenas love their fate far from our lives
love them without reserve
run toward the center of the galaxy that is in the depths
where the relative makes chaos bearable
and the light is within us and outside of us
at the same time

we shall seize by force the roots of the day
no creature shall again refuse us
we shall be blessed by the memory of the atom
in a new era.

The Humanist Chaplain Watches Her Daughter Walking through the Herb Garden

T.D. Walker

> "in time's womb / begins all ending."
> —Ursula K. Le Guin, "Hymn to Time"

Each time I bring
you to the herb garden,
let you wander while
I write some eulogy,
some blessing, I catch
how you watch me, your hands
light on the edge of a balm
leaf: you stop me to ask

why here, why this garden,
always here, and I give
you the only answer
I've ever given: because
it reminds me most of home,
my parents' semi-rural
backyard, the balm not this
balm but the peppered seeds
of some wild plant I'd
never learned the name for—

I know your question
will unfurl into what you
want to ask me: why here,

Being into being:
are time and self-
in-this-state and place
some consolation?
In knowing
this delicate forward
pulsing, as if time were a
metaphor for what

we can't have?
You won't answer
me, because you're what
I will become: you
a mother with a questioning child,
places I'm bound to, but can't see.
One thing I'll turn to
perhaps, or what I'll know is
needed to connect us, and
that is out of reach

is that we keep going back, we
will use the same beautiful things you'll
explain this place to me through:

why this hollowed asteroid,   *a sprouting seed, a budding leaf,*
not Earth, why wait and meet   *wonder caught up in wonder, caught*
my father here, why raise me   *up in our ways of looking at ourselves.*
aboard this ship—   *How can we see the world*
And I will write the answer   *as anything else, but as potential,*
into some eulogy, some blessing, *some time we'll have anywhere?*
watching you slip between   *Your memories of other places*
these green rows, too   *will keep me, and I'll pass them*
orderly to be a home. Your   *home to those to come. Plant a*
finger curling leaf-like   *seed like this momentum, and*
back into itself and then out   *I will follow. Tell me of home*
again, beckoning me to follow—   *and I will come home.*

Couch Burning

Tania Pryputniewicz

Behind the farmhouse it waits,
cushions stacked over kindling
beside a red can of gasoline and two wives

of friends who hadn't left the commune yet
come to say goodbye, casseroles in Corning Ware
rimmed with cornflowers and gold rootlets

of baked oil. I loved it still—its coarse maroon velvet
prickling palm, bald canvas paths my fingers trace:
massive leaves to stem where pattern began again,

hours reading the Le Guin book the parents argued over
behind closed door, then to my face, then gave in,
in which the *he* doubles as a *she* in certain seasons to lie

with a lover, something warm to cling to, soothed
by their foreign worlds while this one breaks down
night after night, fabric singed off frame,

morning's coiled black springs
welded fast in a row like sisters,
ribs exposed, circling over the coals.

My 1980

Stephanie Burt

It was now my younger brothers who had
philosophical objections to taking a bath.

After I came back from the optician,
gold backs for earrings, aglets and fish scales,

erasers' edges, girls' clean fingernails,
were no longer fuzzy, a probability cloud,

but evident in separate outlines, sad
as Atari pixels with their 8-bit math.

I had not the means but the active imagination—
so adults said—to go anywhere: for example,

into the Earth's hot mantle
in a box elder bug-shaped burrowing ironclad.

I was the stowaway on an Edwardian liner
who showed what the locket's ancient pictographs meant,

thanks to my prior study of Egyptology,
delighting the princess by proving she was not cursed.

I was also the unaccompanied minor
afraid to look down, or out at the Atlantic,

as we began our rickety descent
toward Fort Lauderdale-Hollywood International Airport.

I thought of myself as omniscient, as ichthyomantic.
I wanted to spend the following week immersed

in sea-floor adventures, a Nebula-winning tetralogy,
or swimming, as a kind of last resort.

On Reading Le Guin

Mary Soon Lee

Yesterday I packed my bags,
said goodbye to husband, daughter,
cats, friends, the daily chores,
told my son to hurry up
if he was coming too.

Before we left the house,
before we opened the door,
I smelled salt in the air,
heard the wind whip waves
against the wooden wharves.

Years since I last sailed
the islands of Earthsea,
but everything the same:
the swift hawk's flight,
that brightness on the water,
the fire the dragons woke in me.

The boy I met thirty years ago
glanced past me, eager for adventure,
his impatience pinned in the pages
with his youth, while I,
outside the story for so long,
had grown older, fatter, named my son,
but now am coming home.

Earthsea

Bernard Horn

In the first great scene of the story
the boy Ged reveals and exhausts himself
conjuring up fog and managing to dismantle it
into ghosts that harass the blood-
thirsty invaders who chase
the taunting shapes he has fashioned
over a cliff and plunge to their deaths,
in cold damp smoke. Thirty years ago
I read my youngest daughter this book, now
a gift from her to her nephew
on his ninth birthday, for me to read again,
this time grandfather to grandson as he curls
his lean body into mine as if we were exposed
to South Pole weather on some old expedition
and our huddle was our only way
of surviving the ice. The great scene today is neither
the snowboarding the aunt and nephew
threw themselves into earlier this day
at the Snow Bowl in Vermont, nor another grandchild
singing the Queen of the Night at seven,
seven thousand miles away in her Mediterranean city,
but rather a rare moment in an alternate reality,
Le Guin's, early in Earthsea, when good and evil
for once are sharply distinguished
when the great balance of all things
has not yet been revealed.

Time Is Being and Being Time

Eva Papasoulioti

In response to Ursula K. Le Guin's poem "Hymn to Time"

And Chronos said, Let there be time
And tied a red string from the moon to the sun,
     deep in the crevices of existence.
And asked the waves to measure the escape
      from the hurry of the cosmos.
And taught the wind how to kiss the vacuum,
    the silences,
            the imagination.
And showed the birds patterns to trace their dreams
     with atemporal intuition.
And bathed the trees in shades of sequence
     their life a ring of tactile thought.
And Chronos interwove breath with words, with lilies
     And joined hands with light and darkness.

Lessons from Mother

Lynne Sargent

Do not fear escape.

In darkness, in places of fear,
sometimes our duty is to abandon
all other duties, to bury,
to leave.

Feel no shame in clinging to light.

Accept a rescuer, accept that doing so
is no small triumph, that to walk
into the future, still afraid of both
present and past, does not make
your body one of cowardice.

Respect your voice.

It is important. Today it might save
the life of a child. Tomorrow,
it might coax a dragon from the heavens,
but first, you must support it with your breath,
and even if you do none of those other things,
that breath will be enough.

Embrace change.

Even if the only way to enact it,
is in imagination.

A Metaphor of Sparrows

Erin K. Wagner

> *adveniensque unus passerum domum citissime pervolaverit*
> —Bede, eighth century

adveniensque unus passerum domum citissime pervolaverit
the sparrow, a needle, threading from death and birth to life and death.
thus one relates the words of a man dead and in his history *resurrexerit*
adveniensque unus passerum domum citissime pervolaverit
a pagan king in front of a raging fire deciding the merit
of grasping a post-life clarity, a knowing after last breath
adveniensque unus passerum domum citissime pervolaverit
the sparrow, a needle, threading from death and birth to life and death

and entering, a single sparrow flies quick through the hall
high among the rafters, life and flight pinioned between sill and sill.
as if she hears the wild winds of a night beyond life call
entering, a single sparrow flies quick through the hall
and exits again into snow and wind that closes round its thrall
with the same intensity of cold mercy as before touched to kill.
and entering, a single sparrow flies quick through the hall
high among the rafters, life and flight pinioned between sill and sill.

adveniensque unus passerum domum citissime pervolaverit
and high among the rafters, life and flight were pinioned between
    sill and sill
below, a pagan king in front of a raging fire decided the merit
of that sparrow, who, *adveniens, domum citissime pervolaverit*.
he grasps for the likeness, as his councilors call it

between the birds who fly and the men who walk,
the sparrow who flew quick, *citissime volaverit*,
and he, who sat before the fire, unhastening, to talk.

5. The Farthest Shore

Journey

Lyta Gold

Grief keeps its own timetable.
You never know when it's arriving
or departing, leaving behind
a socketed emptiness, a space
where the sea wind breathes
in, out
the harsh music of the gulls.

If you asked me to say
a few words about Le Guin—
I'm not sure I have them.
Read her: it's all there.
I think she died with few words left unsaid—

though never perfectly,
I believe she would have said,
never the true hard place,
the irreducible stone of pain,
the kingless kingdom found,
the leaf-light silence mapped,
the alien decently met,
and all the dragons named.
But that's the sweet impossibility of artists,
dreaming shrines to their own dreams,
an illustrated atlas of eternity.

I read *The Tombs of Atuan* when I was nine,
in a fever, very sick,
sometimes it seems
I'm still wandering that labyrinth,
the eaten girl striving against death,

the devouring ones
that leave everyone else alive, unfinished, in grief.

In the imperfection of artists they leave us
signposts, tickets, breadcrumbs,
a path and nourishment for the journey,
the next iteration of the mysteries.
And when at last, wandering,
you find the place
where the demons lie defeated,
momentarily at least,
in the lap of the priestess-child
you ask,

"Is this right?"

and she smiles
and she gives you a ticket for the next train.

Dragon Haiku

Mary Vlooswyk

One of Ursula's comments I love is when she was asked whether or not she believes in the dragons that she writes about. Her reply? "People who deny the existence of dragons are often eaten by dragons. From within." I think of her at family dinners during holiday season, where I never know what may arise!

holiday dinner
sleeping dragons
awaken

The Ineffable

Valeria Rodríguez

Between the rocks of the sea Tranquility
listen from abysmal distance
the unmistakable voice
of the viridiana with vertices too sharp
the loud howls
a hectic road with fugitive stars
in the margin, the surge of saffron from the craters
the stopped pulse vibrates, the crumbs of the west are eaten
everything that is known: animals and vegetables,
the beloved, the hated, the ignored
he discovered wrinkles festooning the cardinal points
feels his blood is burning
the waves of the sphere are silenced cosmographies
trembling forcibly
unknown and silent in his wild destiny
the lands where magicians live
disappearing in an eyes' close
like the names that can not be revealed
like dragonfly
when the day is over

Cat's Canticle

David Sklar

If you speak I will not answer,
if you call I will not come,
if you throw things at my shadow
I will nail them to your thumb.

You can call me by a name
that you are quite convinced is mine,
but the name by which you call me
I left out for you to find;

the name that guides my hand I carry
locked inside a box,
in an egg, inside a sparrow,
in the belly of a fox.

If you speak I will not answer,
if you call I will not come,
if you throw things at my shadow
I will nail them to your thumb,

but when you call the name that I have
crafted out of clay,
I'll catch your breath inside a bottle,
sealed with wax to make it stay.

Reincarnate

Kate Boyes

Sun glows on drooping hemlock tops
as a drowsy bear cruises the forest edge,
scratching her back on wild rhododendrons,
scattering pink petals on the dark pond below.

Hunger drives her past thickets of blackberry,
huckleberry, salmonberry, thimbleberry,
their fruit still too small, too green.

Hunger drives her, and memory,
something from before the long-sleep,
a gnawing drawing her to this cedar grove—

this place of sap-smell-flicker-sound-duff-feel—
to dig into buried nests of bumblebees
and gorge on their tart taste-sting.

Her claws craft stories of death and desire,
tales told in dirt piles drizzled with fresh saliva,
and in clouds of dazed bees that buzz-zing nearby.

At dusk, she picks the latch on a bear-proof bin,
feasts on fat salmon skin and brioche crumbs,
licks the last dribbles of sticky sweetness
from a carton of Tillamook ice cream.

Spring

Nisi Shawl

This is the first poem I ever wrote. It's very short. I wrote it when I was six. Ursula liked crows, so I think of her now when I read it.

One of my favorite memories of Ursula is of going to lunch with her and her husband, Charles, and my friends Vonda N. McIntyre and Eileen Gunn. We had just finished taping an interview with Ursula (it's still available online and was included in Arwen Curry's documentary *Worlds of Ursula K. Le Guin*). We left the recording studio by the back door and traipsed through an alley past a big green dumpster, disturbing three crows at their own lunch of garbage. Not the most picturesque scene. But Ursula remarked sagely on their intelligence and lifted the moment from squalor to glow.

It's spring:
the crows are singing,
and the old ladies are wearing new hats.

Note To Ursula K. Le Guin

From JT Stewart in Seattle

"Memory demands so much,
it wants every fiber
told and retold."
  Denise Levertov

I.

On growing old
you once said
"the names go first"

perhaps   perhaps
but not yours
not yours

This note w/out postage
cannot be folded   copied
seduced by carrier birds

This note conjures itself
from inside out
not from top to bottom

This note sidesteps time

II.

Shall we gather at the river
the Snake River in Oregon
in the valley of Chief Joseph's
beloved Wallowa Mountains

Should we dip our fingers
in the cold waters
touch the petroglyphs
the Nez Perce carved

Yes

Watch my spirit self
summon my ancient
Native American kin
from these stones
these waters

Watch me
Watch me

Behold all this
from a summer
annual writing workshop
the Fishtrap Gathering
in Wallowa Lake, Oregon
where / when
you recommended me
as a teacher

III.

So
Ursula K. Le Guin
what you gave us
remains

So
from you
now as a werewoman
on the moon
your wish prevails

Keep on
keep on giving us
your voice
your wit
your wisdom

'Nuff said
JTS

Oregon: Local News

Tricia Knoll

Waves of bluster rain roll down the blacktop hill.
People at the coast fled a tsunami but here
it's rain and chances for more rain: 100%,

as if the sky knows that Ursula Le Guin
is gone and we'll be left with her worlds
apart, a few cats, and first-edition books

we bought because they took us away,
saved not to start a pricey collection;
some things we never let go.

We took medical care into our own hands
and voted big-time to tax hospitals and insurers
to keep Medicare for people who need the most,

have the least, and from whom much was taken.
In the women's locker room, talk took today to
old ladies' pot parties with lessons

on what works best, the reason being
that if the old Oregon ladies are willing to stand up
to the feds, by god, someone better listen.

Ursula was one of us.

There Must Be Darkness

Catherine Rockwood

In a dream, my father saw my youngest son
coming down a slope on his push-bike,
as fast as lighting.

This dream happened in winter.

I ran to catch him, my father said,
but Toby was always ahead,
a dim light collecting on his pale, short hair
as he flew over hill after hill:
they were low, and brown, my father said, the landscape unchanging
in its seemingly infinite extension.

Then, he said, *I boarded a train to catch him, but missed—*
and I have been on that train too
in the continual absence of other passengers
as it halts and rattles through sprawling tessellated cities
toward conjunctions arrived at far too late.

I didn't know what to feel, as my father related his dream:
sadness, maybe, at the absence of a linking function
that would allow us to speak together
of a place we had both been alone in. Fear
maybe. Fear, certainly. I thought,
"who could I trust, to interpret this dream?"
My child coasting bravely, by himself,
all that long descending way
with the light in his hair
and my father struggling after.

Later, I was angry, because I had been sad and afraid
alone, while my father laughed and told his dream.

When he finished, I said, "your dream reminds me of
The Farthest Shore,
by Ursula K. Le Guin."
He said he hadn't read it.
We kind of moved on.

I couldn't say more then. If I had
it would have been a yell, CAN YOU NOT SEE,
but he couldn't—
well, the dream was terrifying in several directions.
I don't blame him now.

At the time, instead of yelling, I withdrew
just long enough to write the beginning of this poem
while my father minded the children, with my husband.
Writing helped, but it wasn't enough.
"I must reread the book," I thought,
and rejoined my family,
and put Lebannen's journey off
for months.

The feelings would die down, I thought.
They'd be more manageable later, surely.
And the book would stay for me,
Ursula's thoughts would stay for me,
I could go back to them when I was ready;

I wasn't ready. Or perhaps what I'm saying is,
the mistake lay in wanting to be *unmoved*
by what I knew was there, somewhere, in *The Farthest Shore*
which I reread in summer, in a cabin by a lake,
while Toby slept peacefully in the next room
and my husband launched a boat from the stony lakeshore
sailing our older children from island to island
and my father walked alone in the woods
in sunlight and birdsong.

Oh how I cried on that quiet porch, reading.

"That's right," Ursula said, "that's right."
"Now go on, there's more to do."

The Poetry of Ursula K. Le Guin: A Retrospective

R.B. Lemberg

Introduction

Ursula's eighth collection, *Late in the Day*, contains a little gem of a poem, "My Job," in which she contemplates her life as a writer: "I started out as a prentice / at five years old, and at near eighty-five / in most ways I still am one, / being a slow learner. And the work / is quite demanding" (49). Her first piece, at the age of five, was poetry. Her first publication, "Folksong from the Montayna Province," a poem in the Orsinian cycle, was published in 1959, two years before her first short story publication. She sent the revised manuscript of *So Far So Good*, her ninth full-length poetry collection, for copyediting a week before she passed away. Poetry frames Le Guin's body of work and her life.

Yet, Le Guin's poetry is not as well-known as her prose, or even her essays. Le Guin herself remarked upon this discrepancy with frustration. In her essay "The Reciprocity of Prose and Poetry," she wrote: "Although I wrote and published poetry first, my reputation was made as a prose writer, and I find my poetry quite often dismissed" (Le Guin 1989, 109). Le Guin believed her poetry was overlooked because people expected her to write novels, but I feel the reason is slightly different. Readers unfamiliar with Le Guin's poetry often assume that it is speculative, but those who expect science fictional brilliance from Le Guin's poetry will be disappointed. Speculative poetry is not front and center in her poetic repertoire, and science fiction poems are quite rare in her work.

While Le Guin's fiction often has a cosmic scale, her poems excel on the local, personal scale. Her poems highlight the landscape of the Pacific Northwest with its city trees and its wild places, volcanoes, shadows, houses, birds, the street she lived on, her family, her own aging body, the inevitability of death. Le Guin wrote many poems about writing, too, the craft, her frustrations with it, rarely her triumphs. She wrote poems about current politics, mythology, and her own spiritual views, which evolved through the years. Her poems have been overlooked perhaps because they are smaller scale, more intimate, more fragile.

For this retrospective, I embarked on a months-long read-through of Ursula's poetic works. I wanted the read-through to be exhaustive, but although I am very certain I've read most of her poems by now, I am just as certain that I have not read all of them. Le Guin wrote endlessly; some poems are uncollected, and some, I suspect, are still unpublished, in the archives. With nine full-length collections and quite a number of chapbooks, collaborations, uncollected works, and poems included in works of prose, Le Guin's poetry is a significant part of her creative and personal life.

In *Blue Moon over Thurman Street* (NewSage Press, 1993), a collaboration between Le Guin and the photographer Roger Dorband, Le Guin describes walking one street, Thurman Street in Portland, Oregon, for thirty years. As she walked, she noticed the small things, all the permanence and the changes. At Ursula's suggestion, Roger Dorband began to walk as well, for seven years, taking hundreds of photographs. Some of these were included in the book, with Le Guin's poetic reactions. Her projects are retrospective, multilayered, sometimes collaborative—in her poetry, as in her life, she took the long walk. Reading and rereading Le Guin's poetic works, I was taking a long walk along the same street. Just as Roger Dorband's photographs did not quite document what Ursula saw, my walk undoubtedly differs from her own. I took almost forty thousand words of notes along the way; enough for a larger and more academic project, which I discuss in my postscript.

What I share with you today is not a full treatment of Le Guin's poetry but touchstones of my read and reread. My thoughts about her nine major collections are arranged chronologically, with exploration of her major themes. (I mention some, but not all of the chapbooks, due to space limitations.) I hope you will appreciate taking this walk with me.

First Collection: Wild Angels
(Capra Chapbook Series, 1975)

Although her first published work was a poem, Le Guin turned to poetry more fully in her mid-forties. Her first collection, *Wild Angels,* was reissued in 2018 by Copper Canyon Press as part of a campaign to fund the publication of Le Guin's final collection, *So Far So Good* (2018). I read the original 1975 edition.

Wild Angels is a slight volume—it is Le Guin's shortest full-length book of poetry. The book's dedication reads, "In memoriam, A.L.K. 1876–1960." A.L.K. refers to Le Guin's father, Alfred Louis Kroeber, who had died fifteen years prior. The poems therein reflect on family: Kroeber's life, Le Guin's childhood, and her own children. She writes about her writing and—as always—the landscape of the Pacific Northwest. *Wild Angels* is full of trees. In the preface to *The Wind's Twelve Quarters*, Le Guin confessed to "a certain obsession with trees, which, once you notice them, keep cropping up throughout my work. I think I am definitely the most arboreal science fiction writer" (*The Wind's Twelve Quarters*).[1] "Arboreal" (33) is about family ("the family tree has not got back / to trees yet"), and her family poems are often about trees, like the poem "There," in which the trees planted by her father and the trees that grew wild come together in a meditation on grief:

He planted the elms, the eucalyptus,
the little cypress, and watered them
in the long dusk of summer

...

Do you see: there where his absence
stands by each tree waiting for nightfall,
where shadows are his being gone, there
where grey pines that no one planted
grow tall and die... (33)

---

1 *The Wind's Twelve Quarters* was originally published in Perennial Library 1987. The citation is from the Harper Perennial edition, 2004, 97.

Fifteen years after her father's death, the wild pines he had not planted had grown and gone, but grief remains. We live in a society that prizes fast action. We are called to live, write, even grieve faster, but I learned from reading Le Guin's poems that she embraced slowness—including the careful, iterative process of writing about the same themes. In *Wild Angels*, for example, we find the first of her poems about Mount St Helens: "O mountain there is no other / where you stand the center / is" ("Mount St Helens/Omphalos," 43). She continues to write about Mount St Helens after it erupts in 1980, and decades later. Through her poems, Le Guin makes a contemplative place for herself, and for us: "The averted face of absence / turns. There / the years can go uncounted" (17).

Wild Angels is dense with mythmaking. The first and titular poem of the book, "Wild Angels," explores personal mythmaking and the landscape of California and her own life:

> O halfseen passers of the lonely knolls,
> Before all sorrow and before all truth
> You were: and you were with me in my youth.
>
> Angels of the shadowed ancient land
> That lies yet unenvisioned, without myth... (7)

That shadowed, ancient land is perhaps, her own internal landscape: if so, this book lays out the touchstones of personal mythmaking that continue throughout her work: landscape, family, rites of passage, names and naming, women's issues, her writing, and aging. Growing old, her own inevitable mortality, and death are major themes, as well. Her oft-cited poem "Ars Lunga," about the novelist's craft, opens with a somewhat humorous "I sit here perpetually inventing people / as if the population boom were not enough," but it closes with a meditation on death and life:

> I don't want new heaven and new earth,
> only the old ones.
> Old sky, old dirt, new grass.
> Nor life beyond the grave,
> God help me! Or I'll help myself

by living all these lives
nine at once or ninety
so that death finds me at all times
and on all sides, exposed,
unfortressed, undefended,
inviolable, vulnerable, alive. (29)

We witness this vulnerability, this continuous personal unfortressing, through the decades of her poetry.

In *Wild Angels*, as in other works from this period, we see glimpses of Le Guin as a Taoist. In the profound closing poem, "Tao Song," she meditates on "the road" of one's life and creativity. The road can be shown to us by slow fish or bright sun; but it is not a road of personal agency: "if you can choose it, it is wrong. / Sing me a way, O song: / no one can lose it / for long" (50). We cannot choose the right way, but neither can we truly stray from it. This is a reassuring message in a body of work focused on mortality. But later, we will see how she speaks, again and again, about being lost.

Second Collection: Hard Words
(Harper and Row, 1981)

Le Guin's second collection, *Hard Words*, appears six years after her first collection. At 79 pages, *Hard Words* is longer but also more uneven than *Wild Angels*. In addition to new material, *Hard Words* incorporates prior chapbooks: *Walking in Cornwall* (1976)[2] and *Tyllai and Tylissos* (The Red Bull Press, 1979).

The book includes five sections. Of these, the first, "Wordhoard," engages with issues of creativity and craft. In the titular poem of the section, a dragon is reluctant to part with her treasure of words. Le Guin's frustration with the process of writing runs through many of her poetry collections. Time and time again, Le Guin returns to her central themes, often expressing frustrations with this iterative approach, as in "The Mind is Still": "Words are my matter. I have chipped one stone / for thirty years and still it is not done, / the image of the thing I cannot see. / I cannot finish it and set it free, / transformed to energy" (9). The chipping away and chiseling reappears in "The Marrow," wherein the poet tries to pry clear "a word inside a stone," but despite her efforts, she still cannot hear "the word the stone had said." Only after the poet gives up and throws down the stone can she begin to hear its voice: "and as I turned away it cried / the word aloud within my ear, / and the marrow of my bones / heard, and replied" (10). The truest word cannot be forced out with the violence of a chisel, but must instead be listened to.

The second section, "Dancing at Tillai," incorporates poems from the chapbook *Tillai and Tylissos*, co-authored with her mother, credited in the original chapbook as Theodora K. Quinn (a last name from her third marriage). Theodora Kroeber wrote the second section, "Dancing at Tylissos," while the chapbook's first section, "Dancing at Tillai," was authored by Le Guin and reprinted in *Hard Words*. This section focuses on dancing, daughters, and mothers, and I feel that Le Guin was fond of it: a number of reprints from *Dancing at Tillai* appear in the "Selected

---

2   Crescent Moon Publishing reissued the chapbook in 2008 with new color photographs by Paul Evans and Paul Lewin.

Works" section of her seventh collection, *Finding My Elegy*. This section feels uncomfortably appropriative to me—Le Guin is inspired by Indian mythology, with poems like "Śiva and Kama," "Paśupati," "The Night," and "The Dancing at Tillai" (the last two reference the goddess Kali) and others. Le Guin mixes seriousness and humor with self-reflection in some of these poems. In "Epiphany," she reflects on her fascination with Hinduism: "Did you hear? / Mrs. Le Guin has found God. / Yes, but she found the wrong one. / Absolutely typical. / Look, there they go together. / Mercy! It's a colored woman!" (19). The lines of the poems in this section/chapbook are shorter, more dance-like, but also less detailed; she feels less rooted here. Le Guin's interest in other cultures, and often uncomfortable borrowings, reflect her upbringing and heritage (her mother wrote children's books based on Indigenous myths).

After "Dancing at Tillai," I was happy to move on to "Line Drawings," a sparse section with many short poems. This is the contemplative, place-rich Le Guin:

> One must walk
> lightly. This is fragile.
> Hold to the thread of way.
> There's narrow place for us
> in this high place between the still
> desert and the stillness of the sea.
> This gentle wilderness. (36)

Reprinted from an earlier chapbook published privately, the fourth section, "Walking in Cornwall," feels different from much of the rest of the material—the lines are longer, the imagery denser, richer. This is Le Guin's tremendous, detailed, and intricate poetry of place: "The road goes low between walls / of spark-strown granite, dry-laid / by those who cleared the little fields, / and kept up since, for maybe eighty generations" (53). This section has ruminations on the Bronze Age, the Middle Ages, and recent mining history; the poems are about the landscape of Cornwall—the downs, the sea, the heifers, the sheep, the stones.

The last section of the collection, "Simple Hill," contains one extraordinary long poem, "The Well of Baln." It is one of the longest and most vivid speculative poems I found in Le Guin's work: a dark fantasy poem of the highest caliber, written from three viewpoints (Count

Baln's, his wife's, and his daughter's). The poem features a mysterious hole in the center of his house that troubles the Count of Baln:

> And all the leaves and diamonds and hounds
> fall into it, the hours and eyes and words,
> the closer that I clutch them sooner gone,
> and disappear. I lean above the well.
> I call and gaze. No star, no stir. (71)

In the poem's second section, Count Baln's wife remarks that her husband is troubled, but she finds nothing in the room; it's "an empty cellar like a prison cell." She sees her husband go in and shut the door behind him. He comes out without the gold, without the family dog—but "[t]here's nothing there. / Nothing stored; the bare floor; / nothing, nothing to fear" (72).

Finally comes the third viewpoint, that of Baln's daughter: a dark, chilling, and mystical segment all about death. The daughter has

> ...been down that well a hundred times.
> I used to play with children with white hair
> in one of the countries down inside the well
> where all rocks are glass. (73)

She pays the boatman with her father's gold to take her "to the country on the other side" (73); she likes it there. This is a chilling and imaginative poem beautifully executed. Its speculative focus is a rarity in Le Guin's poetic work—although we'll see other fairytale-inspired poems and many poems that focus on death; the boatman and his boat will certainly reappear.

Third Collection: Wild Oats and Fireweed
(Harper and Row, 1988)

The third full collection of Ursula's poetic works, *Wild Oats and Fireweed*, opens with "'Child on Forest Road' by Wynn Bullock," a poem with a curious history. Photographer Wynn Bullock captured "Child on Forest Road" at a ranch near Big Sur in 1958. The child was a boy who lived at the ranch. Le Guin wanted to use the photograph as a cover image, but her editor would only agree if there was some connection between the image and the collection. Thus, "Child on Forest Road..." was written.

There is no surprise as to why the *child* becomes a *girl* in the poem: the poet imagines herself as the child who is beginning her journey in a mysterious forest full of strange sights and sounds. The old woman is perhaps Ursula herself, as she is at the moment of writing, perhaps even older, who is "coming on home" from the forest. But the child and the old woman have not met yet. We will see in Le Guin's last three collections, especially in the final one, *So Far So Good*, that she again writes herself as a child.

This poem feels like it might have been written quickly—the lines are short, the words repeat. Yet it conjures some of the deep, common themes in Le Guin's poetry: it is arboreal, and speaks of women of different ages who encounter each other, and themselves, on vast, silent roads.

The collection is broken into four parts: "Places," "Woman," "Words," and "Women." Le Guin is an expert arranger of her poetry books; their sequences, the number of sections, and the transitions between them are significant. She adopts the four-part Jungian arrangement here and in some of the future collections.

"Northern B.C." is the poem that truly opens *Wild Oats and Fireweed*. It begins with "Land forms / the mind" and ends with "Land informs / mind as water / the hills in working to the sea" (11). This section unfolds with a series of lovely poems of place focused mostly on the Pacific Northwest, but also, surprisingly, on the Midwest. "Three Ohio Poems" incorporates some watery metaphors of the self: "Like that just leave me / alone and I will be welling" (13).

In this section we also find, reprinted in its entirety, her chapbook *In the Red Zone* (1983). Written over three years, these poems depict the explosion of Mount St Helens in 1980 and its aftermath. *In the Red Zone* shows us the mountain erupting: "your virgin crown / is boiling mud, / forestfire, earthshake, / gas, ash, filth, flood, / your breath death. You are / a darkness on the western wind, / a curtain falling for a thousand miles" (19).

Le Guin revisits the site in the next poem, "In the Red Zone," written in October 1981, a year and a half after the eruption. The final section, "To Walk in Here," asks the question, "What's real? Grey dust, / a dead forest./ ... / What's real? / Says the fireweed lightly casting / its words upon the wind" (24). The Red Zone forces one to face that ultimately people do not matter all that much, "[l]ess in the long run / than the fireweed: to the others. / To ourselves we matter / terribly" (24). The final poem in the cycle, "Back in the Red Zone," revisits the place of devastation, but also reflects the impact the event has had on her and how humans have impacted the landscape in the three intervening years. The place is "a word in a foreign language / but recognized / with tears" (26). Perhaps it is a word about the place of humans—even of the narrator—in the ecology of the forest. This wonderful chapbook shows Le Guin's poetry of place. She keeps returning to the themes and sites of prior works, with the same thorough and thoughtful slowness.

Wild Oats and Fireweed is rich in explicitly feminist and woman-centered poems. "The Maenads" hearkens to Greek mythology: when the young women come down the mountain, tired and bloody, to collapse in the agora, the middle-aged women stand watch over them and protect them from harm, just as their mothers have watched over them. This poem fits well with Le Guin's themes of generational continuity of women. Another feminist highlight, "To St. George," portrays the woman as a worm: an earthworm, tongueworm, heartworm, wombworm. "She knows beginnings / and undersides. She knows / the oneworm, the roundworm / unending, hollow, all, egg, / being the dragon" (36)—evoking the dragon poem of *Hard Words* and the dragon's egg.

"The Song of the Torus" is a powerful poem that speaks to Le Guin's experiences as a cis woman in an aging, ailing body: "but I am hollower / having had the very womb excised and being void / in the middle, not the heart of hearts, but there, / where you came from, darling, / reader dear. Including me. / Reciprocal" (67). The poem also evokes the death of Le Guin's mother: "I'm not unmothered yet; / although I brought her ashes home upon my lap, / and took the knife and cut the bleeding part away, / yet the old woman will not sleep. / She mates with bears and stars to find / what may a wombless woman bring to term" (68). Other feminist poems in this collection were less successful for me. I found "The Woman with the Shopping Cart Who Sleeps in Doorways" to be predictable; "The Menstrual Lodge" might be feminist, but it is also appropriative.

One of the central themes of this collection is words and the craft of writing. Standouts include "The Organ," in which Le Guin talks about having a black gland that absorbs words and "transmits them / to nerve and mind / as pure fear" (58), and "Hunger," which ties the theme of looking for the One True Word with her feminist themes.

Another recurring theme is old age. She is only fifty-nine at the time this collection is published, and yet she describes herself as "an old woman talking / in a dark house" (80). In another uncomfortable poem about aging, Le Guin examines her body and finds it lacking: "Replacement of cheek by jowl, / of curve by hook or crook. / Moles, warts, wenlets, cancerlings, / a distressed finish, constellations, / ... / pied beauty—there is none / that hath not some Strangeness / in the Proportion" (82). But while her body has aged, she can still find refuge in her still-endless mind.

The titular poem of the book, "Wild Oats and Fireweed," is about her writing, her relationship with the land, and with America, where "The wild oats, even, are foreign" (55). She talks about her intimate relationship with California, with its fireweed "by the roadsides / flowers, in clearcuts and burns / and wastes of St Helens" (56). Her journeys are iterative: "I return, I turn, I turn in place. / I am my inheritance" (56). The poem concludes with an invocation, "May I before death / learn some words of my language" (57), a sentiment that recurs in her poems.

Fourth Collection: Going Out with Peacocks
(Harper Perennial, 1994)

Le Guin's fourth full-length collection comprises poems written between 1988 and 1994. Like *Wild Oats and Fireweed,* the book contains four sections. The first section, "Fire, Water, Earth, Breath," begins with a series of contemplative nature poems focusing on the Pacific Northwest and beyond. In "The Pacific Slope," the imagery of wild oats hearkens to previous poems and collections. The mountains of the Sierras and the Cascades are seen as "vast sweeps / and westwards slidings down to wild oats and oaks / in valleys" (6).

In this section, too, we find whimsical poems about cats and birds. This might be the first collection where animals take center stage, but we will encounter more animal poems later. "From Lorenzo" is a charming poem from the viewpoint of a cat who transforms into a tree and flies away: "My wings bear me from the bough / so lightly, and I feel / ... / my leaves playing with the wind" (12). The poet's love of both cats and trees really shines through here. Other poems in this section focus on birds. "Buzzard Visit," one of the concluding poems of the section, blends nature with one of her major themes, death. This poem is stunning, with lines like:

> ...I am not dead,
> yet, but it waited
> to see what I was doing.
> Look, I said, I'm sewing!
> But it knew we're all, whatever else
>
> we might be doing, dying. (14)

The concluding poem of the section is "Sun Setting at Cannon Beach," a nature poem that turns to her frequent theme of knowing, or searching for, the true Word or Name:

> My old tongue breaks in two
> knowing the left word and the right word

but not the loud word of ocean
or the great light word. (17)

The nature poems here are spectacularly accomplished—tighter and more precise in their craft than many of the nature poems in *Wild Oats and Fireweed*. Each poem leads to the other gracefully.

The second section, "Fury and Sorrow," opens with "Riding the Coast Starlight." Le Guin is a master of transitions between sections: the first poem of the new section echoes the last poem of the previous one. The poet observes pelicans rising "from the waters of the morning," continuing the watery theme of the ocean. The lyricism soon pivots to heavier themes, foreshadowed in the last line: "white writing on destruction" (21). The poems in this section focus on the world's wrongs, discussing a wide range of issues from national politics that destroy "the Libraries, the Public Schools; the dream / of a republic of the mind is undermined" ("Processing Words," 22), the AIDS crisis ("In that Desert," 24), the injustices and failures of the US justice system, the Hiroshima bombing, and more.

In this section, as in many of Le Guin's poems of this period, the juxtaposition between (cis) men and (cis) women is relentless. The men are the politicians, the corrupt judges, the torturers, protected by rights that do not seem to extend to women. "The Hands of Torturers" is a dark and striking poem that talks about the hands of (presumably, cis) men who torture people, then take a piss; the torturers' hands can be tender, they can "fondle breasts, part labia. / From one body to another / how easily the hands can go" (25). Women, on the other hand, are often portrayed as powerless, silent, or even dead, as in "Cry No More," a poem about domestic violence against women. The poet commands the reader to:

Tell me her name.

Tell me her name and I will build a wall
of the names of the dead
killed in the long war (28)

My favorite poem of this section, and perhaps the whole book, is "Werewomen." It speaks of older women who are afraid, who think about death, who want not to be afraid, who want to be free:

> But listen, there's a moon out there
> and I don't want sex and I don't want death
> and I don't want what you think I want
> only to be a free woman. (26–27)

This poem, which reflects Le Guin's own experiences of her woman-hood and her aging body, feels more viscerally powerful to me than many of her political poems that focus on the news. In general, her political poems feel less nuanced than her nature poems, less striking, and also less personal, as if she gleaned them from watching TV. The lack of focus on intersectional issues, especially race, in these poems troubles me. For example, "Her Silent Daughter," dedicated to Tawana Brawley, discusses the injustices of the justice system and clearly alludes to Tawana Brawley's trial, but it does not mention race at all.

Two other pieces in this section are troubling to me on the axis of race, imperialism, and colonialism. In "The Vigil for Ben Linder," the poet supplies an explanation that Ben Linder was "killed in 1986 by 'contras' while working as an engineer in a volunteer group bringing electric power to villages in Nicaragua" (37). Ben Linder is a white man, and the metaphors the poet uses, of "bringing light" to a "dark country," feel imperialist to me in a way that is not deconstructed in the text:

> To bring light
> to flower in a dark country
> takes experts in illumination,
> engineers of radiance.
>
> Taken, taken and broken. (37)

I am also troubled by "Fragments from the Women's Writing," which is a gorgeous series of poems about the discovery of "elderly women in Hunan who used an ancient script, written and used exclusively by women" (39). The preface explains that Le Guin wrote these "imaginary translations" based on a newspaper article about the discovery. Later, she says, she saw the publisher announce the translations of the actual women's writing.

> Daughter: these are the characters
> forbidden by the Emperor.

These are the bone words,
the cracks on the under-shell.
This is the other grammar. (41)

The poems are short and moving, but I feel it is necessary to consider that Le Guin, a famous white woman writer, published her "imaginary translations" of these women's words before the actual translations were published. As a result, many Western readers would first discover the existence of Nüshu through Le Guin's work. The series concludes with a stanza in which the women writing in Nüshu imagine the women of the future who would discover their writing.

When *Going Out with Peacocks* was published, there were still women proficient in this system living in Hunan; the last woman proficient in Nüshu, Yang Huanyi, died in 2004. There are also multiple works by Chinese artists inspired by the discovery of Nüshu. (Sofia Samatar's poem in this collection offers an in-depth consideration of this exact issue.)

Unfortunately, this approach reflects Le Guin's background as the daughter of white anthropologists doing research about Indigenous cultures; her upbringing conditioned her to write—often powerfully—about other cultures, often without a deconstruction of real-world power dynamics or consideration of who would be silenced or othered by this approach.

The third section, "Kin and Kind," showcases poetry written for people in Le Guin's life. Highlights include "Dreaming California" (for Charles), a wonderful nature poem in which the poet experiences landscape with her husband: "A great oval opened in the dream sky, / full of perfectly ordinary people / with musical instruments, not playing them. / I called you to come out on the porch and see" (50). This is a lyrical and intimate poem, wistful and warm. Another warm and intimate poem is "For Judith (Judith Barrington)": "If you said a word for its softness, / you might say *billowy*, / or *valley floor*, or *lesbian*" (51). Barrington is of course a lesbian poet; she and Le Guin later co-edited a chapbook, *Explaining Flight*, with poetry by other women writers (1997).[3]

The last section, "Dancing on the Sun," is heavy in surrealist and dream-inspired poetry, leading the reader into the spiritual and

---

3 *Explaining Flight*, edited by Ursula K. Le Guin and Judith Barrington (Jan 1, 1997). Flight of the Mind Writing Workshops for Women, Portland, OR.

metaphysical realm, in which the sun stands for eternity. "Bale's Mill in the Napa Valley" (69) begins a series of works about the sun:

> The wheel of the summer night
> turns, and the stone of the sun
> hovers like a golden fly
> above the nether stone.
> Everything is always. (69)

Other poems, like "Sunt lacrimae rerum" are contemplative, brooding; the world is full of tears, inexplicable emotion. "You leave the house / with tearstreaked windows / to walk on a huge, / angrily sobbing hill" (70). In "A painting," "The land lies dark as sleep is / between dreams: formless / matter of forms" (72). There are poems about aging and the writer's craft ("If I puzzle you / I puzzle me" [80]). Death, and Le Guin's anticipation of death, rises to the surface in this section.

Another striking and difficult poem about death is "What I Have."

> I have seen a doomed hawk in a high tree
> mobbed by shouting crows and gulls
> look into silence, silent,
> being hawk being hawk only till death. (81)

"What I Have" leads us to the last and arguably best poem of the collection, "The Hard Dancing," in which the sun is a place of sleep and dying, and eternity:

> Dancing on the sun is hard,
> it burns your feet, you have to leap
> higher and higher into the dark,
> until you somersault to sleep.
>
> ...
>
> the valleys of the sun are deep
> and even brighter deeper down. (82)

I feel that Le Guin is best in these nature-, aging-, and death-themed poems, which are the strongest poetically, the most deeply felt.

Fifth Collection: Sixty Odd
(Shambala, 1999)

Le Guin's fifth poetry collection, *Sixty Odd*, focuses on aging, nature, and memory, with a smattering of political and feminist poems. The collection departs from the four-part structure of the two previous collections, with only two parts. Part One, however, is broken into four sections, and it is a more standard Le Guin collection in composition. The second part, "The Mirror Gallery," feels almost like a mini-collection rather than a part of a whole.

For the first time in a poetry book, Le Guin adds a preface discussing her process as both a novelist and a poet. For novels, she does not borrow characters wholesale from real life; she must first "compost" them. Poetry, however, is different:

> It seems to me that the connection of poetry with experience
> is more immediate and intense than that of prose, yet more
> oblique and mysterious—altogether more paradoxical. And that
> our poetry is often less inventive, more literal, than our fiction.
>
> ...
>
> What I wrote [*in The Mirror Gallery*—RBL] was
> autobiographical but certainly not an autobiography. I couldn't
> choose the subjects. The memories were as self-willed as the
> words. I wasn't in charge. I couldn't even follow, only wait. Only
> those who wished to come would come, and most of them were
> the dead. Some of my people wouldn't show me their face, but
> wore a mask; for these, and those still alive, I used invented
> names....

My father and brothers are scarcely mentioned, my husband
and children not at all. The selection from the past is partial,
following a way of its own towards a discovery that remains
obscure. Getting older, we're likely to get used to following
paths in the dark. (IX–XI)

Part One is titled "Circling to Descend," an allusion, I feel, to aging. This section begins with a simple and resonant poem about starting over: "I begin again at sixty-one. / ... / I try to be true. / I lie and I / begin again" (3). As in other collections, nature poems anchor the story. "A Circle in a Drought" uses drought and dryness as another metaphor for aging:

> Somewhere in this country
> of dry furrow and hard hill
> the scabbed ground cracks
> to a deep blade of shining,
> a bright upwelling,
> mud, rush, mess, hurry of voices,
> the run, the flood, the telling.
>
> ...
>
> I must learn to live drily.
> What to carry. What to leave.
> What to drink instead of water.
> What to wash the dust away with.
> What to listen to. Wind
> will tell me what to say.
> Stone will lead me to beginning. (6)

The last line, "Stone will lead me to beginning," circles back to the first poem of the collection; aging is a circular process.

The theme of circling back resurfaces in "Redescending," a poem about women's rage, with an Orpheus-like figure torn apart by wild girls; later, Euridice pieces him together and instructs him to follow her, and he does,

> A long way in silence
> by the dry sea with one shore,
> a long way without turning
> to the place of returning (8)

This is a feminist poem, but at the same time, it is a poem in which the woman leads the man back to the beginning, the place of births and reversals, where they are united. This journey reminds me of *Tehanu*, originally published in 1990 (Atheneum).

"When there aren't any" is another strong poem about aging and the craft of writing. What can one do when the words do not come, when there's "no echo dogging / the syllable"—nothing to do but "suck the mud and wait." At the end of the poem, Le Guin asks a Grandmother to teach her both the weaving and "the words to be said" (9). The words she searches for are expressed, perhaps, in "Read at the Award Dinner, May 1996": "The poet's measures serve anarchic joy. / The story-teller tells one story: freedom" (11). Freedom and joy are found in poems honoring and following Gabriela Mistral and learning her language (12–13)—delighting in landscape, translation, words, and travel. "Flight 1067 to L.A." is a lovely little poem about the pleasures of air travel before TSA, and a rare mention of science fiction:

> ...I drink white wine staidly
> above the Great Valley in the belly
> of a silvery pseudocetacean
> sailing the airsea to a palmy city.
> I am my ancestors' sci-fi. (23)

However, by section three of "Circling to Descend," the poems turn to themes of silence, a world in which humans and their words are inconsequential: "With or without us / there will be the silence / and the rocks and the far shining" (27). This section contains political poems inspired by the news, exploring the extinction of animal species or the evils of consumerism.

In "Appropriation" (31-2), the poet muses whether it's appropriate to mourn a fledgling acorn woodpecker killed by a Steller's jay. This grief is juxtaposed to the world's sorrows ("Men bomb undefended cities. / Torture. Prison camps. Dead forests.").

The word *appropriation* in this context is striking and uncomfortable, especially in the context of other, political poems that feel far removed from her life:

> So I name this death, as birds do not,
> and women do, appropriate it,

make it my own: the little one that had
no chance to fly. (32)

"October 11, 1491" (34) is an anticolonialist poem that feels un-comfortably colonialist at the same time. It warns Indigenous people to hide and not to greet the ships, using colonialist vocabulary like "old" and "new" world, and Othering phrasings like "timid and smiling" to describe Indigenous people.

"Lost Arrows and the Feather People" is quite powerful, but likewise uncomfortable. It juxtaposes gorgeous nature imagery with the mod-ern winner/loser mentality. The nature stanzas feature birds of different kinds and offer a beautiful foil to the stanzas about political/human fol-ly, which attempt to deconstruct problematic cultural assumptions, but end up feeling inappropriate and othering, to the extent of using slurs.

The fourth section of "Circling to Descend" opens with "The Hill Yoncalla," a found poem composed from letters and diaries by and about a woman called Rozelle Applegate Putnam, who came to Oregon in the first wagon train in 1843. I wonder how much Le Guin thought about these "pioneer" women as she was building up to "The Mirror Gallery," in which her own family's women made similar journeys.

This section, too, has powerful poems about old age and retrospec-tion. Obviously, this topic bothered and occupied her. She felt old at sixty-odd, and before, we saw her feeling old in her late forties. "A Blue Moon: June 30" (52–53) is a bare and cold poem about aging and want-ing to do more—to write more? There's a hunger here to "begin and sing," which returns us to the beginning of the collection; but, by the end of the poem, "north and silence eat the old." She blames her age for her writing struggles. The next poem, "Repulse Monkey," is an import-ant piece that speaks about Le Guin's difficulties:

How I fear and fear to find
which is the year, the month, the week,
so that each movement of my mind
turns me away from what I seek,

that balance point, that backward chance,
the avoided center of the dance. (54)

Le Guin has written about dancing as a creative process before, and dancing as her life; in this piece, she speaks about having missed some pivotal juncture in her creative work, or perhaps consciously making the choice to avoid or turn away from the center. Over and over, she returns to this theme of longing and missed chances.

"Calling" and "Will the Circle be Unbroken?" are poems about relatives, generations, and death, including her own, culminating in "Anon," a poem about her mother. These poems lead us into the second part of the collection, "The Mirror Gallery."

An often difficult section, "The Mirror Gallery" contains twenty-six poems about people from the past who were important in her life and who came to her in a process of contemplation envisioned as a gallery of mirrors.

We learn about Le Guin's childhood from these poems, the childhood spent in her parents' house, "among the friends and visitors / and refugees and anthropologists" (61). It is "the summer country" (61), seen from a viewpoint of a child who does not contemplate the privilege of her academic upbringing, the economic stability of her family, and its settler roots. The poems mention a parade of guests, often academics and their spouses, among them many interesting women. One of them, a child psychologist, a friend of her mother's, is described as "formidable," "a childless woman whose mind was full of children" (60); other people in the poems also appear childless. From her child viewpoint, Le Guin talks about her older female relatives. In *Wild Oats and Fireweed*, Le Guin called herself a "daughter of immigrants" (23), but in "The Mirror Gallery" we find her grandfathers (a grocer, a clockmaker) and their wives, her grandmothers Phoebe and Mimi, as part of a white American story.

Aunt Betsy, the sister of Le Guin's grandmother Phoebe, is described with tenderness; she lived a complicated life as a "pioneer" moving West. We learn of Aunt Betsy's brother discovering, then losing, a fire opal mine. There's a sense of adventure in her stories, but also an unacknowledged colonizing undercurrent.

In "The Gallery," we also find startling, heartfelt poems about childhood friends, their fights and games. There is an awareness, through a child's viewpoint, that some of her friends' lives are much harder than hers. There are poems about her first kiss, teenage crushes, a horse called Tony, beautiful friends whose lives ended early through hardships or illness. There are stories of hardship, adventure, loss, and heartbreak, but these are other people's troubles, not Ursula's, until she reaches college. Here we find a poem titled "College," where she describes her affair with a graduate student who was

"my instructor in the course
in what a woman is
to be. And the vocabulary. (83)

In short, bare lines, she describes how the affair has gone sour:

Next he started teaching me
why women have abortions.
I wanted to drop that course. (83)

This is the first, but not last time in her body of poetry that she mentions having had an abortion. This poem skirts around difficult issues; in the end it focuses on her lover, his privilege, his lessons of misogyny:

...he taught me
that he didn't need anything I had,
because he had tenure
at a very old, exclusive college.
So I learned my lesson.
And I paid the tuition.
And I was graduated
without honors. (83)

Other poems from the college days describe more crushes, friends struggling with addiction, female housemates terrified of college boys who held "a panty raid." With one possible exception, the people in "The Mirror Gallery" seem to be overwhelmingly white and straight— this seems to have been Le Guin's milieu in early life.

The concluding sequence of poems, beginning with "At Oakley," circles back to her family. The lines become longer and more elaborate as these poems focus once more on place. Back at Oakley, she looks for her Aunt Betsy's house, but both the house and the orchards are replaced by bedroom communities.

The poet looks for her mother next in "The Door," to no avail; the mother is not in the Mirror Gallery, and neither is Ursula: "The mother is the door / but not the mirror. / My mother's daughter and my daughter's mother, / still I look, look for her" (95). The last poem, "You, Her, I," is also about the poet's mother—it's a long, thoughtful, painful poem that elegantly follows the previous one.

> How can I come to you
> who never left?
> Bereft, ungrateful, I must turn away
> to make the mythic distance true. (98)

Sixth Collection: Incredible Good Fortune
(Shambala, 2006)

In her sixth collection, Le Guin got tired of seriousness—many of the poems here are whimsical, playful. She wrote some of these poems when she was a participant in the writing group affectionately titled "Poultry." There are some gems in this collection, some painful misses, and some poems are simply romps—it's clear that she is having fun. This collection also contains weighty, serious poems that continue the themes she explored previously (aging, the writing journey, nature, even a return to Mount St Helens). Thanks to the many fanciful poems here and a certain lightness and fearlessness of approach, this collection feels *fresh*, even though Le Guin still explores her darker, heavier themes.

The collection opens with "The Old Lady," a poem about old age that is different in tone from previous poems on the same subject. This one is rhymed, whimsical, and a bit wild, and the first stanza is especially wonderful:

> I have dreed my dree, I have wooed my wyrd,
> and now I shall grow a five-foot beard
> and braid it into tiny braids
> and wander where the webfoot wades
> among the water's shining blades.
> I will fear nothing I have feared. (3)

"I will fear nothing I have feared" feels programmatic for the collection—a departure from previous fear, a fear of stagnation, of wordlessness. Here, we find chuckling birds, a self-deprecating poet suffering from writer's block, and some lovely fairytale retellings. In a Little Red Riding Hood retelling, the girl and her granny are swallowed by the Wolf. They play music inside his gut—the girl on the drum and the granny on the sax—until the heroic Woodsman liberates them. All accolades go to the hero, as expected in a patriarchal society, but the poem's ending is as whimsical as it is wistful:

He smiles modestly; they cheer;
  and I trot home alone,
and nobody will ever hear
  Little Reddy Ridey Roodey on the
    drumbarumbarumba
    and Great Gut Granny on the alto saxophone. (13)

In "The Woman in the Attic," the poet confronts her struggle with writer's block head-on and with self-deprecating humor.

I am the mad woman in the attic,
professionally frantic. Hear my laugh?
…

My heart is not in this poem.
How could it be? My life
is contingent, like that of the Golem
or the Golden Calf,

on a word written on my forehead
or a popular belief.
I am boring, I am bored.
Ha ha I say to joy, ha ha to grief. (11)

It takes great courage to admit to feeling both boring personally and bored by the act of writing; it is a rebellion against the world that measures her worth, and even her life, by her ability to produce writing: "My life / is contingent / … /on a word written on my forehead" (11). In the delightful "The Woman in the Basement" (14), she speaks of herself as "the old old old old woman / dug halfway into the ground" but still ends the section on a triumphant note.

The second section, "Season and Place," opens with the titular poem "Incredible Good Fortune," a California poem that relates to Ursula Le Guin's own feeling that she has both been blessed and "dryhearted." We have already seen dryness as a metaphor for old age and for writer's block. The poet waits for rain that finally arrives in the winter of her life:

O California, dark, shaken, broken hills,
bright fog reaching over the beaches,

madrone and digger pine and valley oak,
I'm your dryhearted daughter. (17)

Digger pines, volunteer trees of the Northern California landscape, crop up repeatedly in her poetry; digger pines are her old woman trees. Another notable poem is "November Birds," featuring geese, crows, and juncos. Here, Le Guin unleashes her linguistic and poetic creativity; geese, for example, are described as "skyhounds, south-streamers, / wild hearts over house roofs, / shivering skeins, broken necklaces, / hundred, hundreds this autumn daybreak / unwriting dark words in long lines" (19). "Another Weather: Mount St Helens" revisits the eruption of Mount St Helens. This is the first formal poem about Mount St Helens, an already deeply familiar place.

Aging and mortality resurface again in "Winter Days": the poet is "so heavy with mortality / I cannot lift my hand / to take the day, but drift and dream" (21). Sleep and dreaming are landscapes of old age; much like in "The Hard Dancing" (*Going Out with Peacocks*, 82), she talks about the country of sleep. This landscape will be explored again in her last and final collection.

Incredible Good Fortune is in dialogue with future books, and her past books, too. "Walking in April" revisits ideas expressed in "The Mirror Gallery." Her aging body is likened to "the soft old shirt / my mother made me seventy years ago" (26):

I wonder, as it wears away to rags
and gauze, will there be a mirror
to see the naked soul in,
or only an unraveling of shadow
as the day widens
and things grow clearer. (26)

The section concludes with an outstanding series of nature poems, including "In Harney County" and "The Cactus Wren," in which hearing the wren is "to draw free from wish and will" (38).

The third section, "Notes from the Cruise," is the least successful part of this book for me. While on a Caribbean cruise, Le Guin writes poems about the places she visits, the local people she interacts with, and her fellow passengers. Most of these poems are technically accomplished, and quite a few are intended as a critique of the colonialist and genocidal history of the region, but ultimately the poems fall short for me, often presenting an othering gaze.

The "we" of some of these poems presents the viewpoint of the white tourists on the cruise, as in "Passengers," which depicts aging or aged passengers as "veterans of the long defeat" in the battle against age; now that they are older and have "blear-rimmed eyes, / wrinkles, bad feet, thin hair, fat thighs" (50), they can go on a cruise, where "nobody has to do the wash" (51)—except for the punchline of the poem: a young brown person who "smiles, and speaks a foreign tongue" (51).

In the section "Sorceries of San Blas," Le Guin repeatedly calls the brown women who labor on producing wares for the tourist trade "witches." I am sure she was going for a playful, positive tone, but it comes across as othering and patronizing. "The Molas" (44) presents a critique of another white tourist woman not respecting the craft of the local brown women, but the poem centers the "lady tourist," progresses to a lengthy, exuberant description of bright wares, and finishes with "tiny, bright-eyed witches"—the local women are almost an afterthought. "Two of Them" (45), another poem that felt othering to me, subjects the brown woman to the white woman's gaze, and the word "little" in the last line feels again both patronizing and dehumanizing. Likewise in "Mementoes," the keepsakes that the tourists carry home from the cruise are "fantasies sewn by fragile dwarves" (55).

A more successful whimsy returns in the fourth section, "Histories." Here we find the delightful poem "Buz," about a fly that peacefully coexists with Le Guin in her house. "Love songs in late May" offers a different love poem for each day (May 22–26), beginning with a song to the cat Archibald. The last love poem is "May 26," which is "no love song" (63)—the poet returns to her previous explorations of death, grief for her mother, and the connection between death and the sun (as in "The Hard Dancing," *Going Out with Peacocks,* 82).

Mortality is also a concern in "At the Feast in the Great Hall," which alludes to Bede's Parable of the Sparrow:[4] human life on earth is likened to a sparrow that flies through a great hall; we know nothing

---

4 Farmer, David Hugh, and Ronald Edward Latham. *Ecclesiastical History of the English People: With Bede's Letter to Egbert and Cuthbert's Letter on the Death of Bede.* Vol. 14. Penguin UK, 1990.

of what went before a person enters this life or after the end of it. ("A Metaphor of Sparrows" by Erin K. Wagner in this collection gives a different take on Bede's parable). For Le Guin, the parable is a chance to contemplate not only mortality, but her recurring feelings of straying and becoming lost. The poet compares herself to a bird that darts through the hall "between dark and dark"; death offers a chance to reconnect to home, which is a place beyond the hall of life:

> My wings
> blundered in brightness, my eyes
> dazzled, then I was across
> and home in wide air and the night.
> Only for a moment was I lost. (65)

This perspective differs from those in previous collections, where she is still trying to find the center of her work in this life. Journeys beyond death are referenced again in "The Lost Explorer": "across uncharted ranges of the mind, beyond / the maps and histories, for rivers no one knows / that leap from undiscovered springs into the sun" (67).

This section also contains some political poems, including "Peace Vigil, March, 2003," "Talk shows," "American Wars," and others, which did not quite work for me. I maintain that Le Guin is at her best when she focuses on nature and lifecycle imagery; her political poems feel more at a remove. When nature and war combine, as in "3/3/03," the result does not always cohere. "3/3/03" begins with a stunning, visceral stanza about the month of March and alders in fog; the second stanza turns to Le Guin's thoughts of war and Roman mythology, and it feels much more abstract, ungrounded. The two stanzas do not ultimately form a satisfying whole.

The last section, "Silence and Speech," focuses on her central themes of aging and dying. It begins with "Invocation." The poet asks silence to find her:

> O silence, my love silence,
> I have feared you: my tongue
> has rattled on my teeth
> dreading to be dumb so long
> when I am done with breath. (79)

This poem speaks to me: I feel that Le Guin begins to make peace with the fact that she veered away from the "aborted center of the dance" of her writing, that she has filled her life with "prattle, / kind blather, and the come and go / of voices, human voices..." She needed that noise at the time, but without silence, she will never be able to hear "the never to be spoken word." She did not want to stop talking, being afraid of falling silent after death. But only through silent contemplation can the "never to be spoken word" be heard. This poem connects us to her other poems about despairing of finding the right word, such as "The Marrow" in *Hard Words*, about a poet trying to chisel the stone to find its word. Le Guin also acknowledges that silence is hard for her in the light-hearted "A Lament for my Poultry," in which she complains about the absence of her poetry group and likens herself to a lone chicken that squats "pecking for a word" after all the other chickens have left (85).

Silence, aging, and the poet's fear of death are explored in "Dance Song," "Seventy," and "Taking Courage." In "Taking Courage," only writing—"a hardiness / of counted syllables" can build "an armature of resonance" that will help her "coward heart" deal with her aging and inevitable death (87). In this last section, Le Guin has largely moved away from whimsy and returned to the cadences developed in previous collections. At the very end, Le Guin is translating Virgil and feels foolish doing so ("Learning Latin in Old Age")—she is still searching for that word she's tried to find all her life, and she acknowledges that Virgil, too, could not find it before the end.

Seventh Collection: Finding My Elegy
(Houghton Mifflin Harcourt, 2012)

Finding My Elegy, Le Guin's seventh full-length collection and her longest, was published when Le Guin was eighty-three. I feel strongly that she intended this collection to be her last and definitive poetry book. It starts with a reprint section featuring a selection from all her major collections and a number of chapbooks; the reprint section is titled "Wild Fortune," the first word from Le Guin's first collection, *Wild Angels*, and the last from her sixth collection, *Incredible Good Fortune*. The poems in *Wild Fortune* cluster around the themes of aging and mortality, and Le Guin's struggles with writing, with finding the true Word. The reprint selection is not necessarily a "best of"; Le Guin constructs an arc that continues in the originals section. The arc is her mortality, and the frustrating search for the center of her writing, with nature as the frame. The collection concludes with a series of elegiac poems about approaching death, all personal, hard-hitting, and mostly bleak.

The originals section, titled "Life Sciences: New Poems, 2006–2010," is further divided into subsections titled after various disciplines. The first is "Socioesthetics," which opens with "Distance." This poem is about distance, but also the way humans pollute the planet, denying distance, "busy filling it / with what we throw out of the car, / paving the house of Shiva with our shit, / scumming Poseidon's silver hair with tar, / fouling the quail's nest" (95). This opening poem about the damage humans do to the environment and to the gods foreshadows the last poem of the collection, "The Conference," which is about gods and human destruction, as well.

Some of the poems in this section explore memory—the memory of material things, such as cheap but beautifully painted porcelain plates bought in Chinatown in 1938 ("Pretty Things," 96)—and of sensory experiences, such as the smell of coal smoke in "In England in the Fifties": "Resinous fragrance of forests / ... / dug out with heart-killing labor, laid on a hearthstone, / lighted. Myrrh on an ignorant altar. Arson of centuries" (97).

We also find political poems, such as "The Mistake" and "The Next War," which will "take place, / it will take time, / it will take life, / and waste them" (101). Another poem about war, "Soldiers," describes how young people are duped into becoming soldiers: "The innocent accept the wrong / That is the soul of war" (104). Compared to such gems as "In England in the Fifties," with its detailed, unusual, and memorable imagery, the war poems strike me as somewhat simplistic, not rooted in experience. I wonder what powerful poems she could have written on these topics if they had touched her life more closely.

"Almost and Always" brings back another theme of Le Guin's—searching for, and failing to find, the right word. It is fascinating to observe how, over the course of these collections, Le Guin constructs this catalog of almosts, failures, near-misses, and losses as a creator even within a career that was so prolific and celebrated.

The second section of original poems, "Botany and Zoology," has some very strong and heartbreaking poems about animals and forests. Here we find her favorites: crows, who "flit like heavy fragments of cast iron, black, / thrown from this tree to that" (120), and trees themselves. There are many impressive poems here, including "Red Alders in March" and "The Greater Forest," an arboreal poem about trees—trees from places and poems past, including a chopped-down horse chestnut described in her chapbook *Blue Moon over Thurman Street* (1993) and the "ancient forests before Rome / and shadowy woodlands yet to come" —all those trees meeting "at root, at deep root" (122). Another highlight of arboreal works in this book is "Pinus Sabiniana," a piece about digger pines, short-lived volunteer trees that grow "fast like a poet or a weed" (124).

> brief pine   grief pine   tear-filled
> beautiful   dear   disregarded tree (125)

Le Guin's attention to dying and disregarded trees in this collection is evocative. The digger pine is the "trash tree   crooked tree   weed tree" (124), and I read this as a metaphor for aging, for human lives, and perhaps even for Le Guin's own work as a poet.

In the same section we find animal poems ranging from light-hearted (like "Grace," a poem about a kitten) to dark poems about struggling and dying animals ("I think of them"). In this series, "Raksha" is a poignant longer poem about a cat in San Jose who lives under an old plastic-covered armchair on the roofless porch. It's a poem about the precariousness of animal lives, of their stubbornness, their dignity, their freedom, and death. Rakhsa, the stray cat, "accepts, she does not beg. / She is wholly respectable" (132). This is a powerful poem and a meditation on how it is impossible to save the animals—at least not without breaking their will, their freedom.

Accepting the mortality of animals is discussed in "At the Clackamas County Fair." Here, the mortality of animals is due to the cruelty of meat-eating humans. It's a memorable and devastating poem.

> ...Splendid,
> feathered bronze and silver, the grand prize rooster
>   crows out his deathsong.
>
> ...
>
> Two goats, their delicate heads together,
>   comfort each other.
>
> White the heifer, fair the girl of twelve or
> thirteen, lying cured in the straw, the heifer's
> drowsy trusting head in her lap; the girl is
>   quietly weeping. (133)

Death is a theme that runs through the third original section, "Meteorology and Geography." The "Mendenhall Glacier" is likened to a cold dragon that dies on the mountain. In the "Measure of Desolation" (136), the "landwind" blows, banishing the rain and recalling dryness as a metaphor for old age.

There are many lovely nature poems in this section, such as "Morning in Joseph, Oregon." These pieces are simple, but they shine; Le Guin's sense of detail and her powers of observation are careful and tender. I often think how many of her readers wanted something else from her, wanted Truths with a capital T, not these small, soft truths. "At Kishamish," a series of poems strung together, is an important work. Rather like "The Mirror Gallery," this series is about memory, but a memory primarily of a place. "The Corner Room I" begins the series of poems, and "The Corner Room II" concludes it:

> A child could climb out the north window to
> the crotch of the big oak whose foliage fills
> the east window. It was a sapling tree
> when this was Betsy's room. Oaks are slow growing. (150)

Having made the journey through the collections with her, the reader will recognize Betsy, and this place, too.

In the fourth section, "Developmental Ontology," the themes of aging and death are developed further. In "At the Center," Le Guin writes about her own center. Her mind is an old house, and she contemplates what an errant hero with a flashlight might find there:

> no minotaur, nothing frightening,
> nothing even to shine his light on,
> only the deep smell of dry grass
> and dry adobe of an August hillside
> when you lie down on it face down
> breathing into and out of that one place
> in the long, kind, warm dusk
> after sunset and before the stars. (151)

This is a death poem, Le Guin's finally reached center, with its dry smells she associates with death, but it's not musty; the very center leads to a place of memory and landscape.

"At the Center" begins a series of death poems. In "The Merchant of Words," a fantasy piece, Le Guin laments the diminishment of her storytelling: she describes how "the seaport city of my years" changed from a rich trading port where her ships returned "laden with wine and honeycomb, / silk, linen, opals, amethysts. / The sailors sang as they rowed in to harbor" (153-4) to the present day, when "Few ships go out now, few come back, and those / are empty, dancing on the waves. / What can I tell you of that other country / from which my caravels return / so lightly" (154). In these and other death-focused poems in this section, the themes of travel and water are repeated. This is a precursor to a longer series about an ocean journey into death in Le Guin's last collection, *So Far So Good*.

The last section, "Philosophy and Theology," opens with the titular "Finding My Elegy," and this poem does not disappoint. Le Guin's poetry is often elegiac. "I can't find you where I've been looking for you, / my elegy," the poem opens. "There's all too many graveyards handy / these days" (173). Having come so close to death, her previous spiritual beliefs are no longer satisfying. She does not want a hero's journey; she is "older than a hero / ever gets. My search must be a watch, / patiently sitting, looking out the open door" (174) until at last she sees a woman who is trying to speak a name. This woman is her elegy:

> My elegy, your clothes are out of fashion.
> I see you walking past me on a country road
>   in a worn cloak. Your steps are slow, along
> a way that grows obscure as it leads back and back.
>   In dusk some stars shine small and clear as tears
> on a dark face that is not human. I will follow you. (174-5)

Many more death poems follow, such as "The Whirlwind" and "Intimations," a beautiful, echoing poem about wanting to cry, crows, and willows. "Some mornings" is a profound poem about waking up each morning: "Breathing the dark air in I almost understand / that soon I would breathe darkness without air" (178). "In the Borderlands" deals with drawing closer to the border between life and death, and saying goodbye to matter; the matter that makes up her body seeks to return to being rock and star:

> Soon enough, my soul replies,
> you'll shine in star and sleep in stone,
>   when I who troubled you a while with eyes
> and grief and wakefulness am gone. (179)

It's hard to read these poems without becoming emotional: these are wintry, rainy poems, and in many of them, Le Guin talks about crying. By the end of the collection, she turns to Classical mythology. These references are frequent in the last two poetry collections, as she is rereading Virgil and thinking about Roman gods. In "January Night Prayer," she evokes Janus, the lord "of winter and beginnings, riven /

and shaken, with two faces, / watcher at the gates of winds and cities," asking him to open her "soul to the vast / dark places" (187). The final poem, "The Conference," features Janus alongside many other deities who gather to discuss what is to be done about the calamities threatening Earth: climate change and wars. This long, mournful poem does not offer much hope until the very end. Despite all the destruction, the Earth perseveres.

This perseverance is perhaps the only solace she has found, too— even after her death, after massive destruction, if civilizations and even most humans are gone, and voices "are few and far between, they are strange voices, / the mouths that speak have changed their shape" (192)—the Earth itself continues.

Eighth Collection: Late in the Day
(PM Press, 2016)

Late in the Day is a slim, slight book. After Le Guin's longest collection, *Finding My Elegy*, the poems in *Late in the Day* feel fleeting. There are no grand death poems here, no definitive final statements—just living. The opening section, "Relations," includes poems about material objects around her: an "Indian pestle," kitchen spoons, earthenware, incense. The objects catalogue her life. These acts of looking and remembering call back to earlier collections. In "Kitchen Spoons," looking at an old spoon sparks memories of her and her husband's "...first apartment, / on Holt Avenue in Macon, / Georgia, in 1954" (5). These poems are small-scale, quieter. We are invited to observe and appreciate the dense materiality and domesticity of a spoon, the process of contemplating objects and their relationships to people.

The theme of relations continues with tree and animal poems that explore connections. "Kinship" (about trees and people) and "Western Outlaws" feature trees that are "despised, rejected, grudgingly accepted" (9)—sagebrush, digger pine, juniper, and scrub oak. We've seen this theme before, in "Digger Pine" in *Finding My Elegy*. "The One Thing Missing" is a gorgeous poem about fireflies returning after a long absence:

> Finally the fireflies came across the Rockies, drifting
> on damp, soft breezes blowing westward
> ...
> to the quietness of California valleys
> where I saw them in a dream from the verandah
> of Kishamish, all the little airy fires
> coming and going in the summer dusk nearby. (11)

The next section, "Contemplations," gathers poems about nature, the sacred, and legacy. "My House," an elegiac and somewhat static poem, is about building a house of the mind that looks out to Eternity: "Above the front door, a word in a language / as yet unknown may perhaps mean Praise" (16).

The idea of Praise reappears in "Contemplation at McCoy Creek," another nature poem, in which the poet envisions Time and Space as temples. There "Self is lost, a sacrifice to praise, / and praise itself sinks into quietness" (17). This loss of self is only an intermediate step. Time and place are deities that ultimately ask for silence from the aging poet, not more words. "Hymn to Time" continues Le Guin's contemplations about time, beginnings, and endings: "the shining, the seeing, the dark abounding" (19). Rounding out this section are poems about legacies of colonialism and natural and human-engineered disasters; the theme of silence continues in some of them, like "Geology of the Northwest Coast."

The next section, "Messengers," shifts into a more mythic mode. "The Story" is a fairytale poem about the shape of a story and its heroes; it uses three gender pronouns (he, she, they) to refer to the different heroes of stories. It's one of the poems that makes me wonder if the poet was having feelings about gender, both binary and nonbinary. The story seems to be a lesson about heroic identity rather than plot. Another retelling is "Hermes Betrayed," alluding to the Orpheus and Euridice myth that Le Guin has written about before.

Le Guin is also increasingly writing about dreams. As she gets older, she spends more time napping or drifting to sleep, and her dreams make way into her poetry. In "The Dream Stone," she searches for knowledge that she had but lost. In "Arion," a dream-guide leads her to see and reflect on her life of creativity, and its ending: "All that's made is in the making: / achieved, completed, gone" (27).

The next section, "Four Lines," gathers some lovely short four-line poems, like:

"Song"

Untongued I turn to still
forgetting all I will.
Light lies the shadow
on the way I go. (38)

In the following section, "Works," Le Guin considers her long career as a writer with such striking poems as "The Games," "To Her Task-Master," and "My Job."

"The Games" likens Le Guin to a racehorse who took the gold earlier in her career, but now the crowds that cheered her on have dispersed. "Do they know how," she asks, "you look at the hurdles, long before you're old, / and wonder how you ever ran that race?" (44). She is not sorry, in the end of her life, to be alone by herself "with nowhere to run, / in quiet, in this immense dark space" (44). But in "To Her Task-Master," a different sentiment emerges. Even at the end of life, the poet still wants to be moved by a higher power to do the work of creativity:

Old as I am, let me before
I get too old to work at all,
work for you a little more.

As in the past, by owning me
    you set me free.
Command my whole obedience,
use my little strength and sense
to shape the end I do not see,
your mystery, my recompense. (45)

"The Games" and "To Her Task-Master" are on adjacent pages, facing each other, and though they express very different emotions, these two opposing pages are the heart of the collection for me. They encompass the struggle of aging, struggling against silence and accepting it, and using her craft to shape the end she cannot see.

"My Job" sums up her life's work from age five to eighty-five. She says she is still an apprentice, "being a slow learner. And the work / is quite demanding" (49). The "boss," perhaps the task-master of the previous poem, "drives the shiny yellow car"—the sun, which is Le Guin's frequent metaphor for the place where the dead go.

The next section is "Times," with spiritual poems about the seasons, the landscape, and aging. In "Between," for example, she uses the metaphor of the seasons to talk about being in-between, between life and death.

The section "The Old Music," begins with an "untranslation" from Goethe's *Nachtgesang*. I am deeply interested in her repeated statement that the new music she sought was not the right one, after all: "The tunes of my own choosing / all sounded false and wrong. / I sought a newer music, / I found an older song" (63). I wonder if by "tunes of my own choosing" she means her political poems? Her newer fiction? I hope that my planned work in the Le Guin archives at the University of Oregon will shed light on some of her process.

In "Disremembering," the poet evokes *Alice in Wonderland*, where surprises and delights may help a weary soul. However, the second and final stanza reverses this hope: "paths long trodden / are lost, the soul plods onward to no end, / fawns, children, flowers, flames forgotten" (64). Unlike the seventh collection, *Finding My Elegy*, where the arc was that of difficult, long, and, in some ways, triumphant death poems that led to the end of a long career, in the eighth collection (and to a degree also the ninth), the poet contemplates that she is still alive and writing but feels weariness and despair in plodding "onward to no end" (64).

In the last poem of the section, "2014: A Hymn," she returns to the theme of praise and the belief that the Earth continues despite every hardship, which she developed in "The Conference," the final poem of *Finding My Elegy*. The Hymn is simpler and less monumental than "The Conference," but I am interested in the recurrence of praise as a theme in *Late in the Day*—this is the third poem that deals with it, and it did not appear in previous collections.

The last section, "Envoi," concludes the collection with a single poem, "The Mist Horse," about an autumn daughter who rides a white wild mare of Iceland, dancing. Le Guin's poetry is full of dancing, but there is much less dancing in the poetry of her late seventies and eighties. It's an interesting way to end the collection that could have been her last.

In a postscript to this collection is Le Guin's much-cited acceptance speech for the National Book Foundation Medal for Distinguished Contribution to American Letters. In it, she talks about production versus art, capitalism versus freedom: "Hard times are coming, when we'll be wanting the voices of writers who can see alternatives to how we live now, can see through our fear-stricken society and its obsessive technologies to other ways of being and even imagine real grounds for hope. We'll need writers who can remember freedom—poets, visionaries—realists of a larger reality" (85). We needed this message at the moment it was published, and we especially need it now.

Ninth Collection: So Far So Good
(Copper Canyon Press, 2019)

The preface for *So Far So Good—Final poems 2014–2018*, Le Guin's last collection, is provided by her daughter Caroline: "Ursula sent off her revised manuscript for *So Far So Good* for copyediting on January 15, 2018. She died January 22. This book, then, is the last collection of her poetry she would edit; it is her farewell." It was bittersweet and moving to read this collection. Like *Late in the Day*, this book is very short, but I feel that it is significant. Everything that is not the core of her poetic work has fallen away. No more political poems about the news. No more second-wave feminist binarist statements about women and men. Le Guin is journeying toward her death. She is a cartographer of her death. The journey has entered its final phase—and it is aimless, rudderless, venturing out into the open ocean.

This book, like *Late in the Day*, has seven sections. The first, "Observations," begins with "Little Grandmother," a tongue-in-cheek poem about an old chickadee who "reproves what's gone amiss" (5). The chickadee is dry-voiced, a metaphor for old age we recognize from other Le Guin collections. This poem adds levity to a collection preoccupied with endings. Although death and dying are front and center here, the collection itself feels serene, not heartbreaking and grand like her seventh collection.

We see Le Guin's quiet focus on death in the way she writes about animals dying. In "Words for the Dead," a mouse is killed by Le Guin's cat, and the poet has words separately for the soul of the mouse and for its body. This poem reflects her thoughts on the dichotomy of body and soul—the body is still, while the soul dances. She is not done talking about dancing, but now it is the dancing of others, not her own, as in the final poem of her preceding collection, where the daughter of autumn dances with the white horse. Here, the mouse's dance is explicitly done only after death.

There are nature poems here, of course. Le Guin often revisits places important to her, and her themes and observations recur, but the moods and seasons change. In earlier collections, for example, she wrote repeatedly about Aprils—by far her most-mentioned month until the last three collections. The nature poems in the latter collections focus on autumn and winter. Even when the pattern breaks, Spring brings with it no renewal. "Six Quatrains," for example, is about October, but also May. One quatrain, "The Winds of May," is about winds that "rustle and sway / making every moment movement" (12). The next quatrain is about May, too, but it's about hail destroying lilacs.

The next section is "Incantations." We are done with the soft first section, and so fortified, we enter the death sequence, which feels to me magical, a ritual. "Come to Dust" is an incantation to the spirit, the dying body which is, perhaps, the poet's own, about to rejoin the circle of nature:

> Spirit, rehearse the journeys of the body
> that are to come, the motions
> of the matter that held you.
>
> …
>
> Fall to the earth in the falling rain.
> Sink in, sink down to the farthest roots.
> Mount slowly in the rising sap
> to the branches, the crown, the leaf-tips. (15)

Even in her death, Le Guin imagines herself as a tree. The theme of rejoining nature continues in "On Second Hill," where Le Guin envisions herself as a little girl, and asks for "these bits of ash and bone / rejoin the earth they always were, / the earth that let her sing her love, / the gift that made the giver" (16). She has written before about the body that asks to be reunited with the elements ("In the Borderlands" in *Finding My Elegy*, 179), but the ending of this poem is gentler. The woman who once was a little girl wants to die, but her craft is celebrated in the end—it is "the gift that made the giver." In "Lullaby," the poet writes again about her child-self. She asks, "where's my little girl at / fleeting away, sleeping away" and though the little girl finds "a way clear away," the poet is still waiting "a day a day an hour a year" (17). She speaks not just of death, but of the long waiting for the last journey.

Le Guin is an arboreal writer, and she is a watery writer, too. The journey she makes toward death is a journey on water. In "Travelers," she talks about the boat that cannot be steered; this boat will appear again before the end. Themes of water and rejoining the cycle of nature continue in "To the Rain," which strikes me as a perfect poem—in form, emotion, mood. It is about the same long journey she is making:

> Mother rain, manifold, measureless,
> falling on fallow, on field and forest,
> on house-roof, low hovel, high tower.
> downwelling waters all-washing, wider
> than cities, softer than sisterhood, vaster
> than countrysides, calming, recalling:
> return to us, teaching our troubled
> souls in your ceaseless descent
> to fall, to be fellow, to feel to the root,
> to sink in, to heal, to sweeten the sea. (18)

The third part, "Meditations," touches upon several themes—observations of objects, judging beauty, a poetry reading. "There is always something watching you" is about being watched by so many things: "A telescope across the city or on Aldebaran. / Your jealous god. Your neighbor's sad desire" (26). The last two lines reveal a deeper truth: "The forest where you've lost your way, / though it knows where you are going" (26). The sentiment echoes her poem at the beginning of *Wild Oats and Fireweed*, "A Child on the Forest Road." In her last collection, Le Guin remains dedicated to tree and root and forest metaphors in which she is lost and made anew.

"Outsight" and "How it Seems to Me" are meditations on death and matter. When I began this project, I assumed Le Guin would be a Taoist all the way through (for more on Taoism in Le Guin's works, including her earlier poetry, see Sandra Lindow's *Dancing the Tao: Le Guin and Moral Development*, Cambridge Scholars Publishing, 2012). In *So Far So Good*, Le Guin has moved farther from Taoism, and her conceptualizations are no longer identifiable with any movement. They have become organically her own:

> In the vast abyss before time, self
> is not, and soul commingles
> with mist, and rock, and light. In time,

soul brings the misty self to be.
Then slow time hardens self to stone
while ever lightening the soul,
till soul can lose its hold on self
and both are free and can return
to vastness and dissolve in light,
the long light after time.
("How it Seems to Me," 30)

The fourth section, "Elegies," revisits her youth. She remembers her parents, experiencing the seasons in the Bay Area, and putting up black-out curtains in Berkeley in 1941. In "Felled," the poet walks through the empty air where once there was a willow. It is a short poem of only four lines, exquisite and poignant. Le Guin excels when she writes about trees, and she's been writing about trees dying, like in "July," where an oak above the barn is

dying a huge branch at a time,
stands in calm mortality, content
with the warm light that has fed its leaves,
the dark waters that have fed its roots. (41)

In *Blue Moon over Thurman Street* (1993, twenty-five years before *So Far So Good*), Le Guin wrote about a traumatic uprooting of a horse chestnut. In *Blue Moon*, the tree deaths are quieter, dying slowly of old age.

The fifth section is "The Night's Journey," which is further subdivided into segments all connected to the cycle of waking, drifting to sleep, dreaming, and waking again. This section prepares us for the next, and pivotal, section of the book: the great journey into the ocean. The segment "Wakeful" begins with "Islanded," one of the many island-themed, watery works here. "Noctis Oceanus" takes us deeper into the theme of boats that set sail into the vast unknown oceans of dying:

If my mind could go on with them
into the compassionless unending night,
boat with no harbor, hunter with no prey (47)

—but she cannot go on that last journey yet. There's wakefulness after dreaming. The next subsection, "Falling," documents the journey into the ocean of death "in a sailless skiff" ("Farther," 50) that is rudderless, with no oars. This image recurs. I feel that, in her mind, she returns to the archipelago, her beloved Earthsea.

She writes more about slipping away into sleep: "The way it comes unnoticed, so easily. / Like when we were on the tide flats / of the great bay, a long time ago now…" ("Sleep," 51).

> There all we know we must know differently,
> in vastnesses, abysses, in shifting images,
> in silences, illusions, monsters, gleams,
> and always, under all, the dark,
> and the peaceful sinking deeper as it rises. (51)

The last two lines are certainly about her death. This poem caps the subsection "Falling." The next subsection, "Dreaming," is short—two poems about the strangeness of dreams, and the people who come into her dreams now, from far away—"traveling over the mountain passes / that nobody living knows. / Old people who smell like fog / and the soft bark of redwoods…. I think they come from home" ("The People," 53). The last subsection, "Waking," only has one poem, "Seaward." It is a poem about dissolving in the ocean, and it's very good craft-wise.

> seafoam my memory
> is also   evanescent
>   spindrift from wave crests
> white manes of the white horses
> blown by the land-wind seaward
>
>   dreams memories all
> becoming immaterial
>   the self unselving
> gone adrift on the same tide (54)

The white mist-horse of the last poem in *Late in the Day* now returns. These repeating images are important; instead of looking for new discoveries, Le Guin repeats the structures. The images and poems recede and return like the surf. So late in her journey, Le Guin is not beholden to the need for novelty or discovery or even an audience—she writes because writing is inseparable from her. She writes about the self unselving, but she is writing still.

With "The Night Journey" section concluded, we enter the sixth: "So Far." Echoing the title of the collection, it is, I would argue, the most important piece; the preceding poems have been preparing us for it.

Le Guin's preface explains the structure of this section, with its twelve poems: "The metaphor (not the subject) of these twelve poems is Lt. William Bligh's navigation of an overloaded open boat four thousand miles from Tonga past the Australian coast to Timor in Maritime Southeast Asia" (57).

This is the last of Le Guin's epic journeys. The first poem, "Planning," sets up departure: "I've lost my ship, / the command I led / and all her cargo. / I have this instead" (57). The narrator is journeying west. The poet is the captain of the boat and the cartographer of the sea of death; she has left the dry land, no more the dryhearted daughter. In the second poem of the sequence, the boat is "Well built but heavy laden / with the weight of our mortality" (59)—a metaphor for her body. The third poem in the sequence, "III. The Food," is an important piece: "Rage was my privilege. / I didn't count its cost. / I've lost my anger / with the rest I lost" (60). What remains is "a hungry patience" (60). The captain and crew dare not come ashore. In "The Absolution," the fifth poem in the sequence, the aging, ailing body is a boat that takes on water.

> Times between responsibilities
> when I am not at the tiller
> or bailing, but can be still for a while,
> the vastness slowly enters deep
> intaken with my breath.
> A quiet attention to all things.
> Unselved. Absolved.
> I wish it could continue so.
> But we are overloaded

and always in danger
and I so need to sleep when I can sleep. (62)

"[Q]uiet attention to all things" is what Le Guin has always had. We see it in her nature poetry, the delicate and unerring attention to detail, the precision and movement of imagery and language. But being this close to death makes her focus tighten. It is her solace, and true center, now that her rage is lost. Like in the earlier poem, the word *unselved* here is significant.

In the fifth poem, we still see the narrator at the tiller and trying to steer but by the seventh poem, "VII. The Course Kept," the ability to steer has been lost. The final destination for Lt. William Bligh's journey is Timor; the metaphorical Timor of the poet's journey is death. (The word *timor* also means "fear" in Latin.) In the eighth poem, "VIII. Timor," the narrator speaks of the greatest fear, which is not death but the loss of consciousness, of the mind: it "is not that landfall: / to lose my way / as I lost my command, / lose strength of hand / so I cannot steer, / the compass of the mind / till no way is left" but drifting aimlessly (65)—perhaps not so unselved after all.

The tenth poem in the sequence, "X. The boat itself," provides a key to all the preceding metaphors of the boat as the body and the self. The "we" of the poem dissolves as well—there has never been a crew. The captain is alone.

The boat itself
the boat myself
alone
my crew my life
that I have never known (67)

The beauty of this poem is that it provides keys not just to the epic "So Far," but to other poems—in previous collections, too—where the boat metaphors have been used. Now that the metaphors have been solidified and the narrator is alone, the precarious, long, unending journey continues: "Between the blazing firmament / and the black abyss we are / in the mercy of the wind" (68). "In the mercy of the wind" repeats at the very end of the poem. The poem "XII. Westering" is last in the sequence, but the destination has not been reached.

From sunrise the wind blows
always to sunset
going where the stars go

my breath the wind

this little boat my body
its ragged sail my soul

going where the stars go (69)

The end of "So Good," and the end of the poet's life, is the journey; she is the cartographer, but the map she gives us lacks the final landfall.

The last section is "In the Ninth Decade." It is lighter than "So Good," letting us out of the book with an exhalation. The poems that open this section are playful; they become darker as the section progresses, but they are easier on the soul than "So Good." In "An Old Novelist's Lament," Le Guin misses herself as her characters: "I miss the many that I was, / my lovers, my adventurers, / the women I went with to the Pole" (75). She writes about looking at old photographs and about the last visit to the house where Betsy once had a room. These poems return us to familiar places, thoughts, and people. She talks about the circuitous ways of time in "Ancestry." In "Walking the Maze" and "Desire and Fear," she talks again about her slow, unsure journey toward death: "Does the way lead out or in? / At the center, or the door, will I be free? / No choices left to make. I follow on / the maze whose gate and goal are mystery" (81). She has not found a unifying personal belief of what happens after she dies.

The highlight of this section for me is "The Combat"—a defiant poem about a battle of rage against despair.

On the farthest margin of old age
in thickets and quicksands of half-sleep
the fat grey serpent of despair
wrestles with the thin tiger of my rage.

The tiger's teeth meet in the snake.
Break, writhing backbone, break! (83)

The last poem of the collection, and the very last poem of this retrospective, is "On the Western Shore," which is a poem about the tides, a poem about Le Guin's long life. Le Guin is a master arranger of words, of collections, and this is a gentler way to end *So Far So Good*, than "So Far," which would be a natural ending for me:

The lowest, the neap tide,
that bares long reaches
that were deep underwater
where the slope grows steep
is when to walk out so far
that looking back you see
no shore. Under bare feet
the sand is bare and rippled. Dark
of evening deepens into night
and the sea becomes sleep. (86)

Conclusion

Le Guin's major collections, read in a sequence, are greater than the sum of their parts. Le Guin wrote poetry for eighty-three years, from age five to age eighty-eight. However, her work as a poet begins in earnest in middle age, with *Wild Angels*, published at age forty-six. As a novelist, she is already acclaimed with her bold, genre- and gender-bending works of interstellar travel, ansibles, anarchy, sharply posed ethical questions, and deep companionships. Her poetry walks a different road—a forest road where the child-self can journey towards the elder-self, the elder-self towards the child. At the very end of her last collection *So Far So Good*, she remembers the words of Yeats, "Soul clap hands and louder sing," and yet it's not what she wanted: "but the song this old soul wants to sing is soft" (86).

She ventures into political topics at times—these poems have their fans, but you, my readers, have seen that I am not too fond of them. They do not feel to me as accomplished as the elaborate, soft voice of the soul that keeps talking about wild oats and tall oaks and discarded, dear digger pines. The poet at forty-six, and fifty, sixty, seventy, eighty, and finally, eighty-eight is the poet who is older. Her big conceptual experiments are not for poetry; much of her poetry is not even speculative. The only kind of speculative work she consistently engages with in her poetry are fairytale and mythic retellings, often Classical.

The subjects recur—Orpheus and Euridice, the Minotaur, little girls wandering through the woods. Le Guin is a poet who retraces her steps, concentric like growth rings on a tree. Recall the poem "Redescending," an Orpheus and Euridice retelling. The journey is made twice. After Orpheus perishes, Euridice must journey to the underworld to retrieve him. She instructs him to follow her "to the place of returning." Only then can the lovers be joined and become one.

> there
> under the roots
> of the hair of the mothers
> in the realm of the maidens

where the unborn surrounds
the womb, and the fathers
dream in the curled
hands of the child who comes to be
in the world, braiding
and twining vibrations
rejoining, and voices
rejoined. (*Sixty Odd*, 8)

The iterations and repeated journeys, re-descents and turns are inten-tional—only through repetitions can the poet explore the deeper mean-ings of her poetry's central themes. The natural world, dying, aging, renewed—the flights of birds, the exploding volcanoes, the slow, patient lives of trees—is the canvas for her emotional life. There are deeper, quieter truths here. I hope you enjoyed making this journey with me.

A postscript. I will continue writing about Le Guin's poetry. This retro-spective essay has morphed into an academic project, tentatively titled "My Old Tongue Breaks in Two: The Poetry of Ursula K. Le Guin." In 2020, I am the recipient of the Le Guin Feminist Fellowship from the University of Oregon to work on this project in the Le Guin archives. As I write this, we are in the middle of a pandemic, and traveling cannot quite happen as planned—but I am hopeful that I will be able to visit the archives soon. Please follow my work at rblemberg.net for updates.

Poet Biographies

Hal Y. Zhang is a lapsed physicist and Chinese/Californian transplant who splits her time between the east coast of the United States and the Internet, where she writes at halyzhang.com. Her chapbook *Sudden Sharp Sunstrokes* won the Heliopolis Chapbook Prize. Recent publications include the language-and-loss chapbook *AMNESIA* (Newfound Emerging Poets Series) and the women-with-sharp-things collection *Goddess Bandit of the Thousand Arms* (Aqueduct Press).

Ursula Whitcher is a mathematician and poet who grew up just outside Portland, Oregon, and now lives in Ann Arbor, Michigan. Ursula enjoys drinking strong coffee, climbing walls inefficiently, and knitting fingerless gloves. Ursula's poetry may be found in journals including *The Cascadia Subduction Zone, The Journal of Humanistic Mathematics,* and *Goblin Fruit,* as well as at yarntheory.net.

Izzy Wasserstein is a queer, trans writer of poetry and fiction. Her most recent poetry collection is *When Creation Falls* (Meadowlark Books, 2018), and her work has been published widely in places like *Clarkesworld, Prairie Schooner,* and *Transcendent 4: The Year's Best Transgender Speculative Fiction.* She doesn't have an ansible, but she does believe in the revolution. You can find her work at izzywasserstein.com.

Jo Walton is the Hugo and Nebula Award-winning author of *Among Others* (2012). Her novel *My Real Children* won the 2015 Otherwise Award (previously known as the Tiptree Award). Thus far she has published fifteen novels, three poetry collections, one story collection, and 2 nonfiction collections. Visit her website, http://www.jowaltonbooks.com, for fiction, poetry, plays, recipes, and her blog.

T.D. Walker is the author of *Small Waiting Objects* (CW Books, 2019), a collection of near-future science fiction poems. Her poems and stories have appeared in *Strange Horizons, Web Conjunctions, The Cascadia Subduction Zone, Luna Station Quarterly,* and elsewhere, and she curates and hosts the radio program *Short Waves / Short Poems.* Walker draws on both her grounding in literary studies and her experience as a computer programmer in writing poetry and fiction. Find out more at https://www.tdwalker.net.

Erin K. Wagner grew up in southeast Ohio on the border of Appalachia, but now lives in central New York, where she hikes in the Catskills and listens for ghostly games of nine-pins. She holds her PhD in medieval literature and teaches literature and writing in the SUNY system. Her stories have appeared in a variety of publications, from *Apex* to *Clarkesworld*, and her novella *The Green and Growing* is available from Aqueduct Press. Her second novella, *An Unnatural Life*, is out from Tor.com (September 2020). You can visit her website at https://erinkwagner.com/.

Margaret Wack is a poet and writer whose work has appeared or is forthcoming in *Strange Horizons*, *Arion*, *Passages North*, and elsewhere. She enjoys good tea, dead languages, and bad weather. More can be found at margaretwack.com.

Mary Vlooswyk is an emerging writer from Calgary, AB. Her poetry was shortlisted for Quattro Books' inaugural "Best New Poet in Canada" contest in March 2018. She placed third in a Canada 150 poetry contest. Her writing has appeared in *Asahi Shimbun, Mothers Always Write, FreeFall, GUSTS, Moonbathing,* and *Wild Musette,* as well as the Haiku Canada anthologies *A NeverEnding Story Anthology, Startled By Joy Anthology,* and *Gift of Silence: A Haiku Tribute to Leonard Cohen.* She is inspired by the statement: Dolphins still believe in us even when we give up on ourselves.

Margarita Tenser is an Australian poet with Soviet roots and a lifelong love of speculative fiction. Their work has previously appeared in publications like *Strange Horizons, Liminality Magazine,* and *Star*Line.* You can find them online as @vonbees.

Ana Tapia is a historical fiction teacher at the Writers Academy in Madrid. She holds degrees in Psychology and Cultural Anthropology. Her published works include "Túnel de espejos deformantes" (Leonor Award, 2006); "El polizón desnudo" (El Gaviero, 2009), a work inspired by her experience as an anthropologist; and "Kiriwina" (Fin de viaje, 2012), after her stay in Sweden, a country with which she has a strong emotional bond. She is also the author of "Vértigo" (Cazador de Ratas, 2018) and the book of science fiction poems "Las ovejas radiactivas de Kolimá" (Cazador de Ratas, 2018). She blogs at cienciaficcionpoetica. blogspot.com and is active on Twitter as @AnaTapia74.

Sonya Taaffe (https://sonyataaffe.com/) reads dead languages and tells living stories. Her short fiction and poetry have been collected most recently in the Lambda-nominated *Forget the Sleepless Shores* (Lethe Press) and previously in *Singing Innocence and Experience*, *Postcards from the Province of Hyphens*, *A Mayse-Bikhl*, and *Ghost Signs*. She lives with one of her husbands and both of her cats in Somerville, Massachusetts, where she writes about film for Patreon (https://www.patreon.com/sovay) and remains proud of naming a Kuiper belt object.

Rachel Swirsky holds an MFA in fiction from the Iowa Writers Workshop. She's won two Nebula Awards and published more than eighty stories. You can find her online at rachelswirsky.com.

JT Stewart, an African-American poet, writer, playwright, editor, teacher, and performance artist, co-founded Seattle's Clarion West Science Fiction Writer's Workshop. She taught creative writing, literature, and film studies at the University of Washington, Seattle Central Community College, and Fairhaven College (Western Washington University), where she helped create the literary publication *Ink Speak*. JT's collaborative work includes co-editing *Gathering Ground: New Writing & Art by Northwest Women of Color* (Seal Press) and *Seattle Poets and Photographers: A Millennium Reflection* (University of Washington Press). She also was a part of the artistic team commissioned to create *Raven Brings Light to This House of Stories*, a permanent installation housed in the University of Washington's Paul Allen Library. Her poetry collections include *Nommo* and *Ceremony*, and her work has appeared in the *Seattle Review*, *Raven Chronicles*, *Seattle Times*, and the *Portland Oregonian*. JT served as a writer-in-residence and board member at Hedgebrook, a private retreat for women writers on Whidbey Island, where a distinguished writer's scholarship has been established in her name.

Nisi Shawl wrote the Nebula Award finalist *Everfair* (2016)—an alternate and happier history of the Congo—and the James Tiptree, Jr.

Award-winning collection *Filter House* (2008). They co-wrote *Writing the Other: A Practical Approach* (2005), a standard text on inclusive representation. Previously their poetry has appeared in *The Moment of Change* (2012) and *Talking Back* (2006). They co-edited the anthologies *Stories for Chip: A Tribute to Samuel R. Delany* and *Strange Matings: Science Fiction, Feminism, African American Voices, and Octavia E. Butler.* In 2019, Solaris published their anthology *New Suns: Original Speculative Fiction by People of Color.* Other recent titles include *Talk Like a Man* (2019) and *A Primer on Nisi Shawl* (2018).

David Sklar lives in a cliffside cottage in northern New Jersey and almost supports his family as a freelance writer, editor, and drug pusher. A Rhysling nominee and past winner of the Julia Moore Award for Bad Verse, he has more than 100 published works, including poetry in *Ladybug* and *Stone Telling*, fiction in *Nightmare* and *Strange Horizons*, and humor in *Knights of The Dinner Table* and *McSweeney's Internet Tendency*. He's also the creator of the *Poetry Crisis Line*, which features new cartoons for poets and poetry readers every Monday and Thursday at poetrycrisis.org.

Lawrence Schimel was born in New York but has lived in Madrid, Spain, since 1999. He writes in Spanish and English and has published over 120 books in many different genres. Schimel's two poetry chapbooks written in English are *Fairy Tales for Writers* and *Deleted Names* (both from A Midsummer Night's Press); in Spanish, he wrote *Desayuno en la cama* (Egales). He has also edited poetry anthologies, including *Ells s'estimen. Poemes d'amor entre homes* (Llibres de l'Index), *Best Gay Poetry 2008* (A Midsummer Night's Press), and *De Chueca al cielo. 100 poemas celebrando la diversidad LGTBI* (Transexualia). A prolific literary translator, Schimel contributes regularly to *Modern Poetry in Translation, Latin American Literature Today, Pleiades,* and other journals. Recently he translated into English the poetry collections *Impure Acts* by Ángelo Néstore (Indolent Books, 2019) and *I Offer My Heart as a Target* by Johanny Vazquez Paz (Akashic, 2019). His translations into Spanish include *Geografía del amor* by Kätlin Kaldmaa (Cuarto Propio), *La caligrafía de la aguja* by Arvis Viguls (Valparaíso), and *Amnesia colectiva* by Koleka Putuma (co-translated with Arrate Hidalgo, Flores Raras).

Lynne Sargent is a writer, aerialist, and philosophy PhD student at the University of Waterloo. Their poetry has been published in venues such as *Strange Horizons, Augur Magazine,* and *Apparition Literary Magazine,* among others. Their first poetry collection, *A Refuge of Tales,* was funded through an Ontario Arts Council Grant, and is forthcoming from Renaissance Press. If you want to find out more, reach out to them on Twitter @SamLynneS. For a complete bibliography, visit scribbledshadows.wordpress.com.

Sofia Samatar is the author of the novels *A Stranger in Olondria* and *The Winged Histories,* the short story collection, *Tender,* and *Monster Portraits,* a collaboration with her brother, the artist Del Samatar. Her work has received several honors, including the World Fantasy Award.

Valeria Rodríguez, Mar. Uruguayan, holds a degree in Literature and a Master's in Human Sciences, with a specialization in Latin American literature. Her poetry has appeared in *Stone Telling, Star* Line,* the *Antología LAIA* (New York), *Antología Metalanguage* (Chile), and *Zonapoema* (Uruguay). Her narratives have been published in *Revista Penumbria, Anthology of Rural Women,* and *Magazin, Mi Mochila.* In 2015 she won the National Prize for Child and Youth Literature for the work *La maldición Waite.* valeriarodriguezmar.blogspot.com

Catherine Rockwood's poetry has appeared in *Psaltery & Lyre, Liminality, Lady Churchill's Rosebud Wristlet,* and *The Head that Wears the Crown,* an Emma Press book of poems about kings and queens. She is a book reviewer for *Strange Horizons* and has written about the author Naomi Mitchison for *Tin House.* She lives in Massachusetts, with her family.

Gita Ralleigh works as a medical doctor and completed a creative writing MA in 2015. She has published short fiction with *Wasafiri, Bellevue Literary Review,* and *Freight,* among others. More recently her poetry has been published online at *Liminality, The Brown Orient,* and in anthologies published by 26 Writers and The Emma Press. Her poetry pamphlet *A Terrible Thing* (Bad Betty Press, October 2020) deals with mothers, daughters, and the figure of the goddess in different cultures.

A graduate of the Iowa Writers' Workshop, **Tania Pryputniewicz** is the author of *November Butterfly* (Saddle Road Press, 2014). Recently her poems have appeared in *America, We Call Your Name: Poems of Resistance and Resilience, NILVX: A Book of Magic (Tarot Series), The Rockvale Review*, and at *SWWIM* . Her *Heart's Compass Tarot Workbook* is forthcoming in the fall of 2020. She teaches at San Diego Writers, Ink and Antioch University's online program Inspiration to Publication. Tania lives in Coronado with her husband, three children, one blue-eyed Husky, and a formerly feral cat named Luna.

Christopher Phelps lives in Santa Fe where he teaches math, creative coding, and creative writing for a Montessori high school. He is both queer and on the autistic spectrum. Early in the millennium he received degrees in physics and philosophy, but Dickinson and the dictionary were earlier loves. His poems have appeared lately in *Beloit Poetry Journal*, *Poetry*, and *The Nation*.

Charles Payseur is an avid reader, writer, and reviewer of all things speculative. His fiction and poetry have appeared in *The Best American Science Fiction and Fantasy, Strange Horizons, Lightspeed Magazine*, and many more. He runs Quick Sip Reviews, has been a Hugo finalist fan writer, and can be found drunkenly reviewing *Goosebumps* on his Patreon. When not hunting Hodags across the wilds of Wisconsin, you can find him gushing about short fiction (and his cats) on Twitter as @ ClowderofTwo.

Eva Papasoulioti is a writer of speculative fiction and poetry. She lives in Athens, Greece, with her spouse and their two cats, and translates words for a living. Her work has appeared in *Uncanny Magazine, Syntax & Salt, Abyss & Apex, The Future Fire*, and elsewhere. You can find her on twitter @epapasoulioti and on her blog plothopes.com.

Aimee Ogden is a former science teacher and software tester; now she writes stories about sad astronauts and angry princesses. She is the author of the novella *Sun-Daughters, Sea-Daughters*, and her short fiction appears in venues such as *Analog, Fireside,* and *Beneath Ceaseless Skies*. With Bennett North, she co-edits the zine *Translunar Travelers Lounge*, which features fun and optimistic speculative fiction.

A.J. Odasso's poetry has appeared in an eclectic variety of publications, both genre and literary, since 2005. Their prose most recently appeared in the anthologies *Hidden Youth* (Crossed Genres, 2016) and *Knowing Why* (Autistic Self-Advocacy Network, 2018), and in the Winter 2017 and Spring 2018 issues of *Pulp Literature*. A.J.'s third poetry collection, *The Sting of It* (Tolsun Books, 2019), won Best LGBT Book in the 2019 New Mexico/Arizona Book Awards and was a 2020 Lambda Literary Awards nominee in Transgender Poetry. Under its earlier title (*Things Being What They Are*), *The Sting of It* was shortlisted for the 2017 Sexton Prize. Their poetry and editorial work have been nominated for the Rhysling and Hugo Awards multiple times. A.J. holds an MFA in Creative Writing from Boston University, teaches at Central New Mexico Community College and the University of New Mexico, and serves as Senior Poetry Editor at *Strange Horizons*.

Brandon O'Brien (he/they) is a writer, performance poet, teaching artist, and game designer from Trinidad and Tobago. His work has been shortlisted for the 2014 Alice Yard Prize for Art Writing and the 2014 and 2015 Small Axe Literary Competitions, and published in *Uncanny Magazine*, *Strange Horizons*, *Fireside Magazine*, *Reckoning*, and *New Worlds, Old Ways: Speculative Tales from the Caribbean*, among other venues. He is also a performing artist with The 2 Cents Movement and the former poetry editor of *FIYAH: A Magazine of Black Speculative Fiction*.

Kiya Nicoll lives in an oak grove in New England with a sprawling family and an assortment of cats. They write, tinker with theology, and are gently fascinated with worlds and stars. They have no idea who on Earth they would be without the work of Ursula K. Le Guin. Intermittent blogging can be found at kiyanicoll.com.

Shweta Narayan was born in India, has lived in Malaysia, Saudi Arabia, the Netherlands, Scotland, and California, and feels kinship with shapeshifters and other liminal beings. Their short fiction and poetry have appeared in places like *Lightspeed*, *Transcendent 3*, Tor.com, and *Strange Horizons*. Shweta's been mostly dead since 2010, but they have a few pieces in the works again.

Linden K. McMahon is a writer, performer, and arts & nature connection facilitator. They hold an MA in Creative Writing & Education and have been published in *The London Reader*, *Gutter*, *Shoreline of Infinity*,

Finished Creatures, and other venues. Their first pamphlet was published by Stewed Rhubarb in 2012, and they toured their full-length spoken word show, *Fat Kid Running,* in 2017–18. As well as writing, they run projects that bring together creativity, ecology, and solidarity. They also love sci-fi books, baking, and making pots. http://lindenkatherinemcmahon.org

So Mayer's poetry collections include <*jacked a kaddish*> (2018), *kaolin* (2015), and *(O)* (2015), and their work has appeared in anthologies including *At the Pond* (2019), *Trans Love* (2019), *Spells: 21st Century Occult Poetry* (2018), and *Collective Brightness* (2011). Their books on cinema include *Political Animals: The New Feminist Cinema* (2015) and *The Cinema of Sally Potter* (2009), and their critical writing has appeared in the *Criterion Collection, Kenyon Review, Film Quarterly, Literal,* and *Sight & Sound.* They work at independent bookstore Burley Fisher Books in London and with queer feminist film curation collective Club Des Femmes. @Such_Mayer

Xian Mao grew up in Salt Lake City but always gets nostalgic for Beijing when it rains. At Yale they found their poetic voice with Jook Songs, an Asian American spoken word group where they learned to challenge systems of oppression through authentic writing. Their short play "Fantasy Roadtrip" was performed in the 2019 DC Queer Theater Festival. They currently live in Baltimore with their partner and two wonderful rats. Since the moment they read the short story, Xian has not stopped thinking of Omelas and walking away from there.

Susannah Mandel is from California, Boston, and Philadelphia, in that order. She has lived and worked in France, Japan, and the Middle East, and is interested in things that are one thing and also another thing at the same time. Her fiction and prose have appeared in *Apex, Strange Horizons,* and the *Massachusetts Review*; her poetry has appeared in *Goblin Fruit, Stone Telling,* and *Lady Churchill's Rosebud Wristlet.* What is genre? What is gender? www.srmandel.com; @susannah_speaks. (At present she does not live anywhere; this is a problem; feel free to contact her if you have any ideas; after all, there is never very much tethering us down.)

Jennifer Mace is a queer Brit who roams the Pacific Northwest in search of tea and interesting plant life. A Hugo-finalist podcaster for her work with *Be The Serpent*, she writes about strange magic and the cracks that form in society. Her short fiction has appeared in *Cast of Wonders* and the anthology *Skies of Wonder, Skies of Danger*, while her poetry may be found in *Liminality*. Find her online at www.englishmace.com.

A.Z. Louise is a civil engineer-turned-writer of speculative things, whose conure keeps them company during the writing process. When not reading or writing, they can be found playing folk harp, knitting, or arguing with their sewing machine. Links to their work can be found at azlouise.com.

Sandra Lindow's critical book, *Dancing the Tao: Le Guin and Moral Development*, was a finalist for the Mythopoeic Award for Scholarship. Lindow is also the author of the Le Guin online bibliography for Oxford University Press (2019). She has authored eight poetry collections. Her poetry can be seen in *Star*line, Strange Horizons, Asimov's*, and elsewhere. She lives on a hilltop in Menomonie, Wisconsin.

Kendra Preston Leonard is a poet, lyricist, and librettist whose work is inspired by the local, historical, and mythopoeic. Her first chapbook is *Making Mythology* (Louisiana Literature Press, 2020), and her work appears in numerous publications, including *vox poetica, lunch, These Fragile Lilacs*, and *Upstart: Out of Sequence: The Sonnets Remixed*, among other venues. Leonard collaborates regularly with composers on works for voice including new operas and song cycles, and her lyrics and libretti have been set by composers including Jessica Rudman, Rosśa Crean, and Allyssa Jones. Follow her on Twitter @K_Leonard_PhD or visit her site: https://kendraprestonleonard.hcommons.org/.

Mary Soon Lee was born and raised in London, but has lived in Pittsburgh for over twenty years. Her two latest books are from opposite ends of the poetry spectrum: *Elemental Haiku*, containing haiku for each element of the periodic table (Ten Speed Press, 2019) and *The Sign of the Dragon*, an epic fantasy with Chinese elements (JABberwocky Literary Agency, 2020). She has a website at http://www.marysoonlee.com and tweets at @MarySoonLee.

Tricia Knoll is a poet riding out the pandemic in the Vermont north woods with two dogs. Her poetry appears widely in journals and anthologies—and much of it is posted on triciaknoll.com. Her recent collection *How I Learned To Be White* received the 2018 Indie Book Award for Motivational Poetry. Her earlier books focus on eco-poetry—interactions between people and wildlife in urban habitat, a small organic farm in Washington state, and change over time in a small town on Oregon's north coast.

Wendy Howe is an English teacher and freelance writer who lives in Southern California. Her poetry reflects her interest in myth, diverse landscapes and ancient cultures. She has been published in various online and print journals, including *Gingerbread House Lit Magazine*, *Eternal Haunted Summer*, *Mirror Dance*, *Strange Horizons*, *Not One Of Us*, *Goblin Fruit*, *Mythic Delirium*, *Coffin Bell*, and *Liminality*. Look for her latest work in *Polu Texni* and *The Poetry Salzburg Review*.

Bernard Horn's book, *Our Daily Words*, received the Old Seventy Creek Poetry Prize and was a finalist for the 2011 Massachusetts Book Award in Poetry. His poems have been finalists for the 2016 *Mississippi Review* Poetry Prize and the 2018 Raynes Poetry Prize. His publication credits include *Dime Show Review*, the *New York Times*, *Home(less)ness: Geographies of Identity: a zine*, *Tupelo Quarterly 2*, and *Devouring the Green: Anthology of New Writing* (2015). Horn's translations of Yehuda Amichai's poetry have appeared in *The New Yorker* and other magazines. His book *Facing the Fires: Conversations with A.B. Yehoshua* is the only book in English about Israel's pre-eminent novelist.

Ada Hoffmann is the author of the space opera *The Outside*, the story collection *Monsters in my Mind*, and Autistic Book Party. She is a finalist for the 2020 Philip K. Dick and Compton Crook Awards. Ada lives with a mixed-up non-neurotypical household in Ontario and works at a university teaching computers to think. You can find Ada online at http://ada-hoffmann.com/, @xasymptote.

Neile Graham is Canadian by birth and inclination but currently lives in Seattle, USA, where she met Ursula Le Guin through her work with the Clarion West Writers Workshop (for which she won a World Fantasy Award). Neile's poetry and fiction have been published in the US, the UK, Canada, and now all over the internet. She has four full-length poetry collections, most recently *The Walk She Takes* and a spoken word CD, *She Says: Poems Selected and New*. For more information, see neilegraham.com.

Amelia Gorman writes weird fiction and poetry in Eureka, California. In her free time she enjoys exploring the forests and tide pools with her dogs and fostering puppies from her first, redwood, house. You can read her recent fiction in *Nox Pareidolia* and some of her poetry in *Vastarien*, *Liminality Magazine*, and *Sycorax Journal*.

Kim Goldberg is the author of eight books of poetry and nonfiction. Her latest work is *Devolution*, poems and fables of ecotastrophe. Kim's speculative poems have appeared in *Dark Mountain Books, Literary Review of Canada, Switched-on Gutenberg,* and elsewhere. She organized and chaired the Women's Eco-poetry Panel at the inaugural Cascadia Poetry Festival in Seattle. Kim lives, wonders, and wanders on Vancouver Island. Twitter: @KimPigSquash

Lyta Gold is the Amusements and Managing Editor at *Current Affairs*, a leftist magazine of politics and culture. She writes sci-fi, fantasy, essays, poetry, and political satire. Her work has appeared in *Current Affairs, Protean,* several volumes of the Sirens benefit anthologies, and the poetry magazine *Keep This Bag Away From Children*. Ursula Le Guin is her favorite writer.

Gwynne Garfinkle is a Los Angeles native, a poet, fiction writer, and erstwhile rock critic. Her collection of short fiction and poetry, *People Change*, was published by Aqueduct Press in 2018. Her work has appeared in such publications as *Strange Horizons, Uncanny, Apex, Cossmass Infinities, Zooscape, Not One of Us, Dreams & Nightmares, Lackington's, The Mammoth Book of Dieselpunk,* and *The Cascadia Subduction Zone*. For more about her work, visit her website: gwynnegarfinkle.com.

Nicole Field (he/she/they) writes across the spectrum of sexuality and gender identity. They live in Melbourne with one of their partners, two cats, a whole lot of books and a bottomless cup of tea. They can be found on WordPress: nicolefieldwrites.wordpress.com and Twitter: @ faerywhimsy.

Thoraiya Dyer is an Aurealis and Ditmar award-winning, Sydney-based writer and veterinarian. Her short science fiction and fantasy stories have appeared in *Clarkesworld, Apex, Cosmos, Nature,* the anthology *Bridging Infinity,* and boutique collection *Asymmetry.* Thoraiya's novels *Crossroads of Canopy, Echoes of Understorey,* and *Tides of the Titans* are published by Tor books. Find her online at thoraiyadyer.com or on Twitter @ThoraiyaDyer.

Roger Dutcher lives in Beloit, Wisconsin. He has been active in science fiction and in poetry since Ray Bradbury appeared in his life. His poetry has appeared in numerous publications including *Asimov's, Modern Haiku, Amazing Stories,* and *Alba.* He was a poetry editor with *Strange Horizons* for almost ten years. He is co-founder of *The Magazine of Speculative Poetry.*

Jeannelle D'Isa sometimes writes poetry and, in other guises, writes queer Regency romances. She couldn't imagine a world without *The Left Hand of Darkness,* but she also holds an immense affection for *Orsinian Tales.* Her short story "Your Fingers Like Pen and Ink" is available as part of the Lesbian Historic Motif Project's podcast fiction series (August 2020). She deeply regrets buying that melodica for her spouse and child.

M.J. Cunniff is a PhD candidate in literature at Brown University whose work focuses on modernist and contemporary poetry, speculative fiction, and the Anthropocene. MJ lives in Providence, Rhode Island, with a dog statue and a haunted chandelier.

Dr. Edmond Y. Chang is an Assistant Professor of English at Ohio University. His areas of research include technoculture, race/gender/ sexuality, video games, RPGs, and LARP, feminist media studies, cultural studies, popular culture, and 20/21C American literature. He earned his PhD in English at the University of Washington. Recent publications include "Drawing the Oankali: Imagining Race, Gender, and the Posthuman in Octavia Butler's *Dawn*" in *Approaches to Teaching* *the Works of Octavia E. Butler,* "Playing as Making" in *Disrupting Digital Humanities,* and "Queergaming" in *Queer Game Studies.*

Stephanie Burt has been called "one of the most influential poetry critics of [her] generation" by the *New York Times.* Her books of poetry and literary criticism include, most recently, *After Callimachus* (Princeton UP, 2020) and *Don't Read Poetry: A Book About How to Read Poems* (Basic Books, 2019). She is Professor of English at Harvard University.

Kate Boyes is the author of *Trapped in the R.A.W.: A Journal of My Experiences during the Great Invasion,* a speculative fiction novel (Aqueduct Press, 2019). Her essays have appeared in many journals and anthologies, including two volumes of the *American Nature Writing* series. She has taught writing at Southern Utah University and for state and national arts-in-education programs, served as Assistant Editor for *Western American Literature,* and worked as a travel writer. She shares her home on the Oregon coast with several bears.

Novelist, editor, and critic **Leah Bobet**'s novels have won the Sunburst, Copper Cylinder, and Aurora Awards, been selected for the Ontario Library Association's Best Bets program, and shortlisted for the Cybils and the Andre Norton Award; Bobet's short fiction is anthologized worldwide. Her poetry has been nominated for the Rhysling and Aurora Awards, and she is guest poetry editor for *Reckoning: creative writing on environmental justice*'s 2021 issue. She lives in Toronto, where she makes jam, builds civic engagement spaces, and plants both tomatoes and trees. Visit her at www.leahbobet.com.

Elizabeth (Betsy) Aoki is a poet, short story writer, and game producer. She has received fellowships and residencies from the City of Seattle, Artist Trust Foundation, Hedgebrook, and Clarion West Writers Workshop. She has a short story in Upper Rubber Boot Books' anthology, *Sharp & Sugar Tooth: Women Up to No Good,* and her *Uncanny* poem "Okuri Inu, or the sending-off dog demon" was nominated for a Rhysling Award. She is overjoyed to be included in this anthology!

Editor Biographies

A queer Latina originally from South Texas, **Lisa M. Bradley** now lives in Iowa. Her poetry and fiction appear in numerous journals and anthologies, including *Strange Horizons, Beneath Ceaseless Skies, Fireside Fiction, Rosalind's Siblings,* and *The Moment of Change: An Anthology of Feminist Speculative Poetry.* Her first collection is *The Haunted Girl* (Aqueduct Press). Her debut novel *Exile* (Rosarium Publishing) is about a hypersexual antiheroine scheming to escape her quarantined hometown. Lisa also served as Poetry Editor for *Uncanny*'s special issue "Disabled People Destroy Fantasy."

R.B. Lemberg is a queer, bigender immigrant from Ukraine, Russia, and Israel to the United States. Their stories and poems have appeared in *Lightspeed's Queers Destroy Science Fiction, Beneath Ceaseless Skies, Uncanny Magazine, Sisters of the Revolution: A Feminist Speculative Fiction Anthology,* and more. R.B.'s work has been a finalist for the Nebula, the Crawford, and other awards. R.B.'s novella *The Four Profound Weaves* (Tachyon, 2020) is available now. In 2020, R.B. was awarded the Le Guin Feminist Fellowship from the University of Oregon Libraries Special Collections and University archives (SCUA) to conduct research on Le Guin's poetry. You can find R.B. on Twitter at @rb_lemberg, and on Patreon at http://patreon.com/rblemberg. For more information, please visit http://rblemberg.net

Reprint Credits

"sound science" by Hal Y. Zhang first appeared in her collection *Goddess Bandit of the Thousand Arms* (Aqueduct Press, 2020)

"Where Are You?" by Jo Walton first appeared at https://www.patreon.com/bluejo.

"Song of the Guardians of the Rainbow" by Ana Tapia first appeared in *Las Ovejas Radiactivas de Kolima* (Cazador de Ratas, 2018).

"The Other Lives" by Sonya Taaffe originally appeared in *The Cascadia Subduction Zone* 6.4 (October 2016).

"On Reading Le Guin" by Mary Soon Lee first appeared in *Uppagus* #27, February 2018.

"Cat's Canticle" by David Sklar first appeared in *Mythic Delirium*, February 2014.

"Keepsake" by A.J. Odasso originally appeared in their collection, *The Sting of It* (Tolsun Books, 2019).

"Speculative Fiction" by Linden K. McMahon first appeared in *Shoreline of Infinity* 11 (2018).

"Oregon: Local News" by Tricia Knoll first appeared in *New Verse News* on January 23, 2018, the day after Ursula K. Le Guin died.

"Galloping Hooves" by Tricia Knoll first appeared in *Stirring*, a 2016 publication of Sundress Publications.

"Atmospheric Inversion" by Kim Goldberg originally appeared in *Front*, November 2008.

"My 1980" by Stephanie Burt first appeared in her collection *Advice from the Lights* (Graywolf Press, 2017).

"Kudzu" by Stephanie Burt originally appeared in her collection *Popular Music* (Fort Collins, CO: Center for Literary Publishing/University Press of Colorado, 1999).

Additional Aqueduct Press Books
from the Poets & Editors

Trapped in the R.A.W. by Kate Boyes, 2019

The Haunted Girl by Lisa M. Bradley, 2014

People Change by Gwynne Garfinkle, 2018

The Moment of Change: An Anthology of Feminist Speculative Poetry edited by R. B. Lemberg, 2012

Marginalia to Stone Bird by R. B. Lemberg, 2016

Writing the Other by Nisi Shawl and Cynthia Ward, 2005

Filter House by Nisi Shawl, 2008

The WisCon Chronicles (Vol 5): Writing and Racial Identity edited by Nisi Shawl, 2011

Something More and More by Nisi Shawl, 2011

Strange Matings: Science Fiction, Feminism, African American Voices, and Octavia E. Butler edited by Rebecca J. Holden and Nisi Shawl, 2013

The Helix and the Hard Road by Joan Slonczewski and Jo Walton, 2013

Through the Drowsy Dark by Rachel Swirsky, 2010

Ghost Signs by Sonya Taaffe, 2015

The Green and Growing by Erin K. Wagner, 2019

Goddess Bandit of the Thousand Arms by Hal Y. Zhang, 2020